# LGBTI: Lesbian, Gay, Bisexual, Transgender, and Intersex Offenders: Selected Resource for Criminal Justice Professionals

## Contents

# Introduction

This annotated bibliography has been developed in an effort to provide current and useful information to correctional agencies regarding the safe and respectful management of lesbian, gay, bisexual, transgender and intersex (LGBTI) offenders. Relying on a best practices approach, this information will enable corrections staff to make better informed decisions about the safety, security, treatment and care of LGBTI offenders by providing academic, cultural and legal perspectives of the issues that make this group unique.

Surveys conducted by the Bureau of Justice Statistics indicate that non-heterosexual adult offenders report higher rates of sexual victimization while in custody. Similar surveys in juvenile facilities show even higher rates of sexual victimization among non-heterosexual juvenile offenders. Similarly, a 2009 research report cited findings that transgender offenders experienced sexual victimization at a rate thirteen times higher than a random sampling of offenders in the same facility.[1] Such evidence indicates that LGBTI offenders are at increased risk for sexual victimization while in custody, and agencies that ignore this may be placing themselves at risk for litigation.

Changes in federal and state legislation, court decisions, settlement agreements and the proposed standards under the Prison Rape Elimination Act (PREA) are all factors for consideration in the management of LGBTI offenders in correctional settings. For example, the proposed PREA standards contain requirements for agencies to conduct staff training on effective and respectful communication with LGBTI offenders and to enhance sexual abuse prevention measures that specifically address this population.

We are confident you can obtain these resources either through the Internet, the NIC Information Center, the authors, or by ordering them. We invite contributions to this list, as well as additions submitted material to the NIC Library, such as articles and training resources.

---

[1] Sexton, Lori, Valerie Jenness, and Jennifer Sumner (June 10, 2009). Where the Margins Meet: A Demographic Assessment of Transgender Inmates in Men's Prisons. Retrieved from *http://ucicorrections.seweb.uci.edu/sites/ucicorrections.seweb.uci.edu/files/A%20Demograph ic%20Assessment%20of%20Transgender%20Inmates%20in%20Men's%20Prisons.pdf*.

# General

Basow, S. A., and J. Thompson. "Service Providers' Reactions to Intimate Partner Violence as a Function of Victim Sexual Orientation and Type of Abuse." Journal of Interpersonal Violence 27, no. 7 (2012): 1225-241.

Previous research on intimate partner violence (IPV) has shown that abuse in lesbian relationships is similar to that which occurs in heterosexual relationships in both frequency and dynamics. The purpose of this article is to explore whether a woman who is in an abusive relationship with another woman receives the same support from service providers as she would if she were in a relationship with a man. An online vignette study was conducted to examine if a client's sexual orientation and the type of abuse that she has endured had an effect on service providers' perceptions of her as a victim and their willingness to accept her as a client. A national sample of 282 domestic violence shelter service providers completed a 10-item questionnaire about a woman experiencing IPV. Scenarios varied in terms of couple sexual orientation (heterosexual or lesbian) and type of abuse (physical or nonphysical). The results indicate that although participants did not overtly discriminate against a woman in a lesbian relationship, they were less likely to perceive her as a victim, and their acceptance of a lesbian as a client was more dependent on their comfort with her than was the case for a woman in a heterosexual relationship. Type of abuse had a main effect on many questions, with physical abuse taken more seriously than nonphysical abuse. Implications for service providers are discussed. [Journal abstract]

Brotheim, Hal. "Transgender Inmates: THE DILEMMA." *American Jails* 27, no. 2 (May, 2013): 40-42, 45-47. Retrieved from *http://www.readperiodicals.com/201305/3014954021.html*

According to the Diagnostic and Statistical Manual of Mental Disorders (American Psychiatric Association, 2000), gender identity disorder is the presence of persistent and strong cross-gender identification. Surveys conducted by the Bureau of Justice Statistics in 2009 indicate that transgender arrestees experienced sexual victimization at a rate 13 times higher than a random sampling of other offenders in the same facility. Our focus is on the potential for victimization, regardless of sexual orientation. The following guidelines should be implemented to ensure that contacts with transgender individuals are professional, respectful, and courteous and will not lead to complaints and lawsuits: * Do not use language that a reasonable person would consider demeaning to another person, in particular language that refers to a person's gender identity, gender expression, or sexual orientation. * Show respect for transgender persons' identity and gender expression, which includes addressing them by their preferred name and using gender pronouns appropriate to an individual's gender self-identity and expression. [Journal abstract]

Brown, George R. "Qualitative Analysis of Transgender Inmates' Correspondence: Implications for Departments of Correction." Journal of Correctional Health Care 20, no. 4 (2014): 334-42. Accessed January 21, 2015. *https://s3.amazonaws.com/static.nicic.gov/Library/029501.pdf*

> "Claims of inadequate health care and safety afforded to transgender inmates have become the subject of litigation. This article reviews 129 unsolicited letters from transgender inmates writing ... to identify their concerns. Among the letters reviewed were reports from 10 inmates who had filed lawsuits naming departments of correction (DOCs) as defendants, claiming inadequate access to transgender health care. Five of these lawsuits have gone to trial. In all of those cases, the defendant settled the matter or was found liable as of the time of this report. Claims of inadequate care for transgendered patients that have sufficient merit to be fully litigated in U.S. courts appear likely to produce verdicts in favor of plaintiff inmates. The information gleaned from reviewing letters from transgendered inmates may alert staffs of DOCs to concerns worth addressing proactively to avoid the costs associated with transgender-related lawsuits" [Author Abstract p. 334]

Ciarlante, Mitru and Kim Fountain. "Why It Matters: Rethinking Victim Assistance for Lesbian, Gay, Bisexual, Transgender, and Queer Victims of Hate Violence & Intimate Partner Violence: A Joint Policy Report by the National Center for Victims of Crime and the National Coalition of Anti-Violence Programs." March 2010. Accessed September 12, 2012. *http://www.victimsofcrime.org/docs/Reports%20and%20Studies/WhyItMatters_LGB TQreport_press.pdf?sfvrsn=0*

> Advocates for the safety of lesbian, gay, bisexual, transgender, and queer (LGBTQ) crime victims and victim service providers need to read this report. Results from a survey of whether LGBTQ crime victims have adequate access to victim services are presented. Sections of this document include: introduction; what we don't know; what we learned—findings; recommendations; and conclusion. Serious gaps exist in "culturally competent service provision" to LGBTQ victims which "compromises the safety of LGBTQ individuals, families, and communities" (p.iii). Recommendations provide strategies for fixing these gaps.

Clem, Constance, Clem Information Strategies (Longmont, CO), and National Institute of Corrections. Jails Division (Washington, DC). *Large Jail Network Meeting, March 29-31. 2009, Aurora, Colorado*, 2009. *http://nicic.gov/Library/023878*

> Contents of these proceedings are: introduction; meeting take-aways in brief; illegal alien programs; proactive discipline, part 2; PREA update; intersex and transgender issues; Legal Issues in Jails--2009; open forum; announcements; LJN business; final meeting agenda; participant list; and index of past LJN meeting topics.

Denson, Bryan. "Transgender Prisoners in Oregon to Get Formal Policy on Intake Procedures." *OregonLive.com,* April 11, 2014. *http://www.oregonlive.com/politics/index.ssf/2014/04/transgender_prisoners_in_orego.html*

> The Oregon Department of Corrections has worked for two years with Basic Rights Oregon to draft a policy on how to screen transgender inmates during intake at Coffee Creek Correctional Facility.

"Department Policy on Ensuring Equal Treatment for Same-Sex Married Couples". Office of the Attorney General. Accessed March 17, 2014. *http://www.justice.gov/iso/opa/resources/ss-married-couples-ag-memo.pdf*

> The policy will "formally instruct all Justice Department employees to give lawful same-sex marriages full and equal recognition, to the greatest extent possible under the law," according to U.S. Attorney General Eric Holder.

FORGE (Milwaukee, WI). 2011. *Criminal Justice? New Fast Facts about Transgender People, Police, and Incarceration.* *http://forge-forward.org/wp-content/docs/fast-facts-police1.pdf*

> Highlights from a survey of transgender or gender non-conforming people regarding their involvement with police and experiences while incarcerated are presented. Statistics are presented concerning: the percentage of individuals having contact with police; how comfortable this population is asking for help from the police; individuals assaulted by the police; the percentage of individuals sent to jail or prison; and the percentage of those assaulted while incarcerated. The survey is called 'Injustice at Every Turn: A Report of the National Transgender Discrimination Survey' which can be found at *http://transequality.org/PDFs/NTDS_Report.pdf.*

"FORGE: Empowering. Healing. Connecting." *FORGE*.  Accessed September 12, 2012.
*http://forge-forward.org/*

> This website, founded in Milwaukee, Wisconsin, was created to provide peer support to the transgender community.  The website includes information on: Anti-Violence, Trans Aging, Wisconsin specific support, and transgender trainings and events, publications & resources, and news.

Gates, Gary. "LGBT Parenting in the United States." *The Williams Institute,* February 2013. Accessed January 16, 2015.
*http://williamsinstitute.law.ucla.edu/research/census-lgbt-demographics-studies/lgbt-parenting-in-the-united-states/*

> This report from the Williams Institute provides demographics for the LGBT parent population.  The population is segmented by: LGBT-identified adults, LGBT adults who have had a child, and adults and children with an LGBT parent.

"Handbook on Prisoners with Special Needs.*" United Nations Office on Drugs and Crime*, 2009.
*http://www.unodc.org/documents/justice-and-prison-reform/Prisoners-with-special-needs.pdf*

> This handbook covers the special needs of the eight groups of prisoners, which have a particularly vulnerable status in prisons" (p.1). The groups of prisoners are those with mental health care needs, those with disabilities, ethnic and racial minorities and indigenous peoples, foreign national prisoners, lesbian, gay, bisexual, and transgender (LGBT) prisoners, older prisoners, prisoners with terminal illness, and prisoners under sentence of death. Each group has its own chapters comprised of: overview; special needs and challenges; international standards; responding to the needs of these prisoners; and recommendations.

Jenness, Valarie. "Agnes Goes to Prison: Sexual Assault and the 'Olympics of Gender Authenticity' Among Transgender Inmates in California's Prisons." 2010.
*http://nicic.gov/Library/026366*

> Issues relate to transgender inmates in California's prisons are discussed. Parts comprising this presentation are: good reasons to study transgender inmates' growing awareness of transgender people in the U.S. and in correctional settings, high profile court cases brought forth by transgender

inmates, legislative mandates, high rates of sexual assault among this population, and systematic and empirical examination of transgender inmates is lacking; California Department of Corrections and Rehabilitation study about transgender inmates major findings regarding demographic profile, aggregate prevalence rate for sexual assault of transgender inmates, prevalence by characteristics of transgender inmates, by prisons, by housing assignments, and by social-interactional-support factors (i.e., lived experiences in prison),and the 'Olympics of gender authenticity' (perceived femininity).

Jenness, Valerie. "From Policy to Prisoners to People: A "Soft Mixed Methods" Approach to Studying Transgender Prisoners". *Journal of Contemporary Ethnography* 39, no.5 (October 1, 2010): 517-553. Accessed September 4, 2012. *http://jce.sagepub.com/content/39/5/517*

This article describes the official protocol and unexpected contingencies that motored data collection for a large scale study of transgender inmates in California prisons for men. The focus is on gender and sexuality as methodological confounds that, surprisingly and productively, ultimately served to shed insight into basic sociological questions as well address the policy questions that originally motivated the research. Drawing on serendipitously collected ethnographic data from a plethora of exchanges with experts, California Department of Corrections and Rehabilitation (CDCR) officials, researchers, and transgender inmates, this article reveals the categorization commitments and processes that permeate the lives of "the girls among men" in prisons for men. In light of these findings, the author argues for the value of adopting what she calls a "soft mixed methods" approach when doing non-ethnographic work designed to inform policy. To do so stimulates sociological imagination and ultimately provides more nuanced, layered, and complicated answers to policy questions while also providing insights into more basic research questions. [Journal abstract]

King, Erica and Maureen Baker. *Respectful Classification Practices with LGBTI Inmates [Lessons Plans].* New York State Department of Corrections and Community Supervision, 2014. *http://nicic.gov/library/029681*

"Lesbian, gay, bisexual, transgender, intersex (LGBTI) and gender non-conforming inmates represent particularly vulnerable populations with unique medical, safety, and other needs. Though some of the concerns and vulnerabilities faced by these populations are similar, transgender and gender non-conforming inmates are distinct from gay, lesbian, and bisexual inmates in important respects. Basic principles of risk-based classification should be applied with LGBTI populations, accounting for unique characteristics that may affect their risk of victimization. For transgender inmates, this includes making individualized decisions regarding gender placement (i.e., whether the inmate will be housed in a facility for females or for males). Reception staff must have clear guidelines allowing for the consistent identification of LGBTI inmates and collecting key information relevant to individualized risk assessment. Like other important characteristics, an inmate's sexual orientation or transgender status will not always be immediately obvious at reception, but can typically be identified with relatively simple procedures" (p. 1). This 60-minute training session explains how to improve the correctional intake and classification process for LGBTI inmates. Contents of this zip file include: "Respectful Classification Practices with LGBTI Inmates: Trainer's Manual" comprised of the following four lessons—Why LGBTI Responsive Intake and Classification Matters, LGBTI Terminology, Implementing Promising Intake and Classification Practices, and Moving Forward; 14 "Myth or Truth" flash cards; and presentation slides."

Leach, Donald L., II. 2007. "Managing Lesbian, Gay, Bisexual, Transgender, and Intersex Inmates: Is Your Jail Ready?" *Large Jail Network (LJN).* Accessed January 16, 2015.
*http://nicic.gov/Library/period315*

> The management of lesbian, gay, bisexual, transgender, and intersex inmates (LGBTI) in a jail setting is addressed. Sections contained in this article are: a terminology lesson; the sexual being -- physiognomy, gender identity, and sexual orientation; and responses in the jail regarding medical care, data systems, security, housing, and clothing.

Legal Aids Services of Oregon (LASO). Native American Program (NAPOLS), Lewis & Clark Graduate School of Education, Counseling. Indigenous Ways of Knowing Program (IWOK), Basic Rights Oregon, and the Western States Center. *Tribal Equity Toolkit 2.0: Tribal Resolutions and Codes to Support Two Spirit & LGBT Justice in Indian Country,* 2013.
*http://nicic.gov/Library/027855*

> "Tribal laws reflect our values as a people, define our collective barriers, prioritize our issues, allocate public resources, and identify eligibility for conferred status and public benefits and services. This Toolkit identifies areas in which existing tribal laws may discriminate against Two Spirit /LGBT individuals. The Toolkit also gives tribal legislators a brief overview of legal and policy issues that impact the equal treatment of Two Spirit/LGBT community members, and offers sample resolution and code language for tribal lawmakers to consider adopting to maximize equality

within their communities. The purpose of this Toolkit is to protect the most vulnerable among us by facilitating the development of tribal laws that ensure that Two Spirit/LGBT people have the same access and opportunities as other community members. By making simple adjustments to laws and policies— such as creating an inclusive definition of family, or extending criminal laws to address hate crimes based on sexual orientation and gender identity—tribal governments can exercise their sovereignty to better protect all of their tribal citizens" (p. 9). This toolkit is comprised of ten chapters: introduction about the toolkit; family—marriage, domestic partnerships and civil unions, and children (adoption, child custody and visitation for Two Spirit/LGBT parents, and child welfare); employment; housing, real property transactions, public accommodations, and public services; education; health care and end of life; bias-motivated (hate) crimes—criminal offenses with bias motive, prohibiting specific actions, enhanced penalties, and bias-motivated crime reporting and training; jury service; law enforcement and corrections— police conduct, prison/jail conditions, and a sample "Equality Protocol for Law Enforcement and Corrections"; and identity documents and name changes.

Lev, Arlene Istar. 2004. *Transgendered Emergence: Therapeutic Guidelines for Working with Gender-Variant People and Their Families*. Routledge (New York, NY).

Theoretical understandings of transgenderism, diagnosis and assessment, and treatment issues are covered. Chapters comprising this book are: the transsexual phenomenon meets the transsexual menace; the legacy' gender variance in history; deconstructing sex and gender thinking outside the box; etiologies' causes and categories; diagnosis and transgenderism' the creation of pathology; learning to listen to gender narratives; transgender emergence' a developmental process; family emergence; transgendered children and youth; and treatment of intersexed people' time for a new paradigm.

"LGBTQ Detainees Chief Targets for Sexual Abuse in Detention." *Just Detention International.* Last modified February 2009. *http://www.justdetention.org/en/factsheets/JD_Fact_Sheet_LGBTQ_vD.pdf*

The sexual abuse of lesbian, gay, bisexual, transgender, and queer (LGBTQ) prisoners is discussed.

"PREA and LGBTI Rights." March 7, 2014. *American Jail Association.* Accessed on January 16, 2015. *http://www.americanjail.org/prea-and-lgbti-rights/*

"Correctional systems that want to aim higher than the basic protections required for Federal funding by going further to prevent and address sexual abuse and harassment behind bars will also affect public safety by improving inmates' prospects for success once released. In this article, [the author discusses] the basic protections for LGBTI inmates that every juvenile and adult correctional system will need to put in place and offer some extra provisions they should adopt to become models of best practice."

Robinson, Russell K. 2011. "Masculinity as Prison: Sexual Identity, Race, and Incarceration". *California Law Review*, January: 1309-1408.

The Los Angeles County Men's Jail segregates gay and transgender inmates and says that it does so to protect them from sexual assault. But not all gay and transgender inmates qualify for admission to the K6G unit. Transgender inmates must appear transgender to staff that inspect them. Gay men must identify as gay in a public space and then satisfactorily answer a series of cultural questions designed to determine whether they really are gay. This policy creates harms for those who are excluded, including vulnerable heterosexual and bisexual men, men who have sex with men but do not embrace gay identity, and gay-identified men who do not mimic white, affluent gay culture. Further, the policy harms those who are included in that it stereotypes them as inherent victims, exposes them to a heightened risk of HIV transmission, and disrupts relationships that cut across gender identity and sexual orientation. Thus, this Article casts doubt on the claim that the policy is intended to and actually protects gay and transgender inmates. [Abstract from journal]

"San Francisco Police Reaching Out to LGBT Community with Safe Havens". *Bay City News*. April 16, 2013.
*http://www.sfexaminer.com/local/2013/04/san-francisco-police-reaching-out-lgbt-community-safe-havens*

This online news article covers the announcement of ten police stations designated as "safe havens" for the LGBT community in San Francisco.

Sexton, Lori, Valerie Jenness, and Jennifer Sumner. "Where the Margins Meet:  A Demographic Assessment of Transgender Inmates in Men's Prisons". Sacramento, CA: California Dept. of Corrections and Rehabilitation; Irvine, CA: University of California, Irvine. School of Social Ecology, 2009.
*http://ucicorrections.seweb.uci.edu/files/2013/06/A-Demographic-Assessment-of-Transgender-Inmates-in-Mens-Prisons.pdf*

"[T]his research provides the first empirical portrayal of a prison population in California that is unique by virtue of being both transgender and incarcerated" (p. 1). Sections of this document include: abstract; introduction; research methodology and data; findings for education and employment, health, sex work, homelessness, victimization, and self and identity; and discussion. Overall, transgender inmates are marginalized from other prisoners.

"Shawnee County Jail Works to Improve Conditions for Transgender Inmates: Intake process, housing arrangements altered at Shawnee County Jail." The Topeka Capital-Journal. December 29, 2013.
*http://cjonline.com/news/2013-12-29/shawnee-county-jail-works-improve-conditions-transgender-inmates*

This article discusses changes in the Shawnee County Jail policies for evaluation, searches, health and medical exams, and housing of transgender inmates. In addition, these changes support meeting the PREA standards to provide inmate safety against sexual abuse.

"Still in Danger: The Ongoing Threat of Sexual Violence against Transgender Prisoners". Stop "Prisoner Rape, ACLU National Prison Project. 2005. Accessed May 22, 2013.
*http://www.justdetention.org/pdf/stillindanger.pdf*

This report provides an overview of the legal implications of *Farmer v. Brennan* for prisoner claims of Eighth Amendment violations and an assessment of changes in conditions for transgender prisoners in the 11 years since *Farmer*." p. 1.

Support, Social Ecology. "Transgender Inmates in California's Prisons: An Empirical Study of a Vulnerable Population | Center for Evidence-Based Corrections." Accessed January 22, 2015.

*http://ucicorrections.seweb.uci.edu/2009/04/14/transgender-inmates-in-californias-prisons-an-empirical-study-of-a-vulnerable-population/*

Copies of overheads are provided for a presentation about issues surrounding the incarceration of transgender individuals. Topics covered include: backdrop for research; six good reasons to study transgender inmates; "transgender" means different things to different communities; major findings of the California prison study; demographic profile; aggregate prevalence rate; prevalence by characteristics of transgender inmates; prevalence by characteristics of prisons; prevalence by housing assignments; prevalence by social-interactional factor (i.e., lived experiences in prison); and beyond prevalence -- further considerations.

"Surviving Prison in California: Advice By and For Transgender Women." TGI (Transgender Gender Variant Intersex) Justice. Last modified February 2011. *http://nicic.gov/Library/026512*

> "This guide was created because trans women imprisoned in the SF [San Francisco] jails expressed a need for detailed information about going to prison or back to prison after not having been there in a long time" (p. 1). This guide is not only extremely valuable for trans women but for those working with them. Being aware of the issues impacting trans women will make it much easier to understand and effectively manage this population. Information and tips are provided for housing and classification, protecting oneself, education and empowerment, dress code, health, and other resources.

"Systems of Inequality: Criminal Justice." Sylvia Rivera Law Project (SRLP). Accessed February 20, 2013. *http://nicic.gov/Library/026489*

> This diagram illustrates how overpolicing and profiling of low income people and of trans and gender non-conforming people intersect, producing a far higher risk than average of imprisonment, police harassment, and violence for low income trans people." It also describes the additional gender-related harms suffered while in the custody of the criminal justice system.

"Toilet Training: Companion Guide for Activists and Educators." Sylvia Rivera Law Project (SRLP). Accessed February 20, 2013. *http://nicic.gov/Library/026504*

> Even though this guide is intended to accompany a video about bathroom access for transgender and gender non-conforming individuals, it is an excellent resource that can be used by itself. It aims to 'start conversations not only about trans bathroom access, but also about the impact of all sex-segregated facilities (shelters, jails and prisons, group homes, drug treatment facilities, etc.) on people who do not fit within gender norms. This is one of the most controversial and important fronts in the struggle to end gender identity discrimination, and [those at the SRLP] strongly believe that community education is the key to dispelling cultural myths and fears and establishing understanding about the struggle faced by those who do not fit easily into existing norms of binary gender' (p. 1). This publication is divided into three parts: I. Education and Discussion--

Talking Points about Gender-Segregated Facilities, Talking Points about Accessible Bathrooms, Discussion Questions for the Classroom, and Activity Ideas for the Classroom or Workshop; II. Data and Information--Gender Neutral Bathroom Survey, Map of Jurisdictions with Transgender-Inclusive Non-Discrimination Laws, and Interview (excerpts) from Maximum Rock and Roll; and III. Doing your Own Work--sample letters for non-gendered bathroom organizing, and Resources for Transgender Activism.

White, Mel. *Stranger at the Gate: To be Gay and Christian in America*. New York, NY. Penguin Group, 1995.

This is the account of a deeply religious man's coming to terms with his gayness and the impact that process had on his life. A former hostwriter for Jerry Falwell, Pat Robertson, Billy Graham, and other religious-right personalities, White offers a compelling story; gay readers raised in a fundamentalist Christian environment will find themselves saying, "That happened to me." [Abstract from the Library Journal]

Wilson, Kate. "Kristina Olvera Says She is a Woman. The Prison System Says He is a Man. The Fight for Justice for Oregon's Transgender Inmates." April 16, 2014. Accessed January 14, 2015. *http://www.wweek.com/portland/article-22429-kristina-olvera-says-she-is-a-woman-the-prison-system-says-he-is-a-man.html*

"Olvera's condition, gender dysphoria, isn't some made-up complaint concocted by a prisoner looking to make trouble. It's a widely established medical and psychiatric diagnosis, for which treatment includes hormones and allowing the subject to live as the opposite sex."

"Winning the Future: President Obama and the LGBT Community". The White House. Accessed July 17, 2012. *http://www.whitehouse.gov/lgbt*

This site contains blog posts, fact sheets, videos, and the latest news on President Obama's initiatives for the LGBT community.

# Juveniles

Brooks, Carol Cramer, Elissa Rumsey, and Kim Godfrey. *National Center for Youth in Custody Fact Sheet*, October 2011. *https://www.ncjrs.gov/pdffiles1/ojjdp/235770.pdf*

> Provides an overview of the mission, objectives, and services of the recently launched National Center for Youth in Custody. The center will strive to serve the range of facilities in which juveniles are placed, including adult facilities that confine juvenile offenders. Emphasizing the rehabilitative goals of the juvenile justice system, the center will deliver training and technical assistance; identify, document, and promote evidence-based approaches to working with youth in custody; and serve as a resource for juvenile justice practitioners, youth in custody, and families. The center will provide training, training curriculums, Webinars, and professional development, among other services.

"California Becomes First State to Crack Down on 'Gay Cures' for Minors." Jurist. Accessed February 26, 2013. *http://jurist.org/hotline/2013/02/ted-lieu-ca-reparative-therapy.php*

> This article focuses on California's Senate Bill 1172, the first law in the nation to ban the reparative therapy known as sexual orientation change efforts (SOCE).

Cianciotto, Jason, and Sean Cahill. *LGBT Youth in America's School 2012*. University of Michigan Press (Ann Arbor, MI), 2012.

> This is an essential guide for anyone working with justice-involved youth. The authors "combine an accessible review of social science research with analyses of school practices and local, state, and federal laws that affect LGBT [lesbian, gay, bisexual, and transgender] students. In addition, portraits of LGBT youth and their experiences with discrimination at school bring human faces to the issues the authors sicuss" (back cover). This book is divided into three sections. Section 1: A Comprehensive Review of Social Science Research on LGBT Youth ad Their Experiences in School: LGBT youth—a critical population; a grave picture of harassment and violence in schools; and profiles of Thomas McLaughlin, "Pat Doe", and Jamie Nabozny. Section 2: A Comprehensive Review of School-Based Practices and Federal, State, and Local Laws and Policies That Affect LGBT Students: federal, state, and local policy interventions; school-based programs and practices; the No Child Left Behind Act and LGBT students; sex education, abstinence-only programs, and HIV prevention; and profile

of Sakia Gunn. Section 3, A Research Agenda to Guide and Inform Future Policy: political and methodological issues affecting research on LGBT youth; the need for research on understudied LGBT populations; conclusion and policy recommendations for making it better for LGBT students; and profiles of Lawrence King and Corey Johnson.

Dvorak, Petula. "Transgender at Five." The Washington Post. Last modified May 19, 2012.
*http://www.washingtonpost.com/local/transgender-at-five/2012/05/19/gIQABfFkbU_story.html*

> This news article and accompanying video cover the story of a child who has been diagnosed with gender identity disorder at the age of five.

Estrada, Rudy and Jody Marksamer. "The Legal Rights of Young People in State Custody: What Child Welfare and Juvenile Justice Professionals Need to Know When Working with LGBT Youth". San Francisco: National Center for Lesbian Rights; New York: Lambda Legal, 2006.
*http://www.nclrights.org/wp-content/uploads/2013/07/LegalRights_LGBT_State_Custody.pdf*

> The legal rights of LGBT (lesbian, gay, bisexual, and transgender) youth are discussed through the use of scenarios that show professionals in child welfare and juvenile justice what they may experience working with this population. This paper is divided into four parts: the Constitutional right to safety-- in foster care and juvenile detention and correctional facilities; other constitutional rights—the right to equal protection, and First Amendment rights; state non-discrimination laws; and conclusion. "Agencies and facilities that provide care to youth in state custody must educate themselves on the needs of LGBT youth and the scope of their civil rights" (p. 11).

"Growing up LGBT in America: HRC Youth Survey Report Key Findings". Human Rights Campaign. Washington, D.C. Accessed February 29, 2013.
*http://nicic.gov/Library/026170*

> Results from a national survey of lesbian, gay, bisexual, or transgender (LGBT) youth ages 13-17 are presented. "The deck is stacked against young people growing up lesbian, gay, bisexual or transgender in America. Official government discrimination or indifference along with social ostracism leaves many teens disaffected and disconnected in their own homes and neighborhoods. With an increase in public awareness about anti-LGBT bullying and harassment and the strikingly high number of LGBT youth who

are homeless, in foster care, or living in high-risk situations, it is critical that we get a better understanding of the experiences, needs, and concerns of LGBT youth." This graphic rich report shows that LGBT youth face a wide range of challenges while also being upbeat and strong.

Hanssens, Catherine, Aisha C. Moodie-Mills, Andrea J. Ritchie, Dean Spade ,and Urvashi Vaid. "A Roadmap for Change: Federal Policy Recommendations for Addressing the Criminalization of LGBT People and People Living with HIV." New York: Center for Gender & Sexuality Law at Columbia Law School. May 2014. *https://web.law.columbia.edu/sites/default/files/microsites/gender-sexuality/files/roadmap_for_change_full_report.pdf*

This report presents policy recommendations for addressing the criminalization of LGBT (lesbian, gay, bisexual, and transgender) people and people living with HIV.

Hunt, Jerome and Aisha Moddie-Mills. "The Unfair Criminalization of Gay and Transgender Youth: An Overview of the Experiences of LGBT Youth in the Juvenile Justice System." *Center for American Progress*. Washington, D.C. 2012. *http://nicic.gov/Library/026431*

"Gay and transgender youth are pipelined into the juvenile justice system at disproportionate rates, often stripped of their basic dignity and civil rights, and treated in a harmful and discriminatory manner once in the system. The current policies and practices of schools and the juvenile justice system overlook gay and transgender youth and perpetuate stigma and bias that can lead to their unwarranted criminalization and unfair treatment" (p. 7). This report aims to clear up the confusion regarding the GLBT population of justice-involved youth, their treatment by authorities, and should be read by anyone working with juvenile offenders. Sections of this report include: introduction; why gay and transgender youth end up in the juvenile justice system' family rejection, homelessness, and failed safety nets, and biased school discipline policies; unfair criminalization by the system' classification as sex offenders, and detention as a default; discriminatory and harmful treatment' segregation and isolation of gay and transgender youth, physical, sexual, and emotional abuse, and unsafe reparative or conversion therapy; conclusion and practical and policy recommendations.

Irvine, Angela. "'We've Had Three of Them': Addressing the Invisibility of Lesbian, Gay, Bisexual and Gender Non-Conforming Youths in the Juvenile Justice System". *Columbia Journal of Gender and Law* 19, no. 3 (2010): 675-701. *http://nicic.gov/Library/026476*

"[M]yths around the nonexistence of LGB and gender non-conforming [LGBT] youths in the juvenile justice system persist, presenting numerous challenges to the equitable treatment of such youths. Juvenile justice professionals need to know that [LGBT] youth exist within the system, and that [LGBT] youth often enter the juvenile justice system for different reasons than straight youth ... Juvenile justice professional need to know the underlying reasons for [LGBT youths'] failure to remain at home, in placement or truancy in order to identify successful alternatives to detention and out-of-home placements or to assign appropriate terms of probation" (p. 677). Sections of this article cover: estimating the number of LGBT youths in the juvenile justice system; detention patterns of LGBT youths; and addressing the needs of incarcerated LGBT youths.

*Juvenile Justice: Advancing Research, Policy, and Practice.* Edited by Francine Sherman and Francine Jacobs. Hoboken. NJ: John Wiley & Sons, Inc. 2011.

Utilizing an interdisciplinary approach, this volume addresses issues surrounding reform in the juvenile justice system. Twenty-four chapters are organized into four sections: framing the issues, understanding individual youth, understanding youth in context, and working for change.  Chapter 8 focuses on LGBT youth and is entitled "Lesbian, Gay, Bisexual, and Transgender (LGBT) Youth and the Juvenile Justice System".

Koeppel, Maria and Leana Bouffard. "The Consequences of Intimate Partner Violence Victimization By Sexual Orientation." Sam Houston State University, College of Criminal Justice, Crime Victims' Institute, February 2014. Accessed April 2, 2014. *http://dev.cjcenter.org/_files/cvi/IPV%20Sexual%20Orientation%20Report%20for %20web.pdf*

This report presents results using data from the National Violence Against Women survey to compare the consequences of IPV in the form of depression, physical health, and alcohol and drug use between heterosexual and non-heterosexual individuals.

"Lesbian, Gay, Bisexual, Transgender and Questioning Youth". Albany, NY: New York State Office of Children and Family Services, 2008. Accessed September 12, 2012. *http://www.equityproject.org/pdfs/LGBTQ_Youth_Policy_PPM_3442_00.pdf*

This policy is designed "to maintain and promote a safe environment for lesbian, gay, bisexual, transgender, and questioning (LGBTQ) youth in OCFS [New York State Office of Children and Family Services] operated residential and after-care programs" (p. 1). Procedures cover: training of staff; resources and policy dissemination to youth; reporting responsibilities and procedures for staff; incident reporting procedures for youth; enforcement; and childcare practices for LGBTQ youth. The OCFS Guidelines for Good Childhood Practices with LGBTQ Youth are also included. These procedures cover: training; disclosure; youth placement; LGBTQ Decision-Making Committee; mental health assessments; substance abuse; medical; counseling; LGBTQ literature and resources; general facility operations; communication and documentation; language and name; clothing; individual bedrooms; hair and other personal grooming; bathroom facilities; search issues; transition/discharge planning; and reporting.

"Lesbian, Gay, Bisexual Transgender, Questioning and Intersex (LGBTQI) Youth." *Policy and Procedures Manual*, n. DYRS-007. Washington, D.C.: District of Columbia Dept. of Youth Rehabilitation Services. 2012. *http://dyrs.dc.gov/sites/default/files/dc/sites/dyrs/publication/attachments/DYRS-007LesbianGayBisexualTransgenderQuestioningandIntersexLGBTQIYouth.pdf*

"The purpose of this policy is to provide a safe, healthy, accepting environment for lesbian, gay, bisexual, transgender, questioning and intersex (LGBTQI) youth, and to prevent harassment and discrimination against youth who self-identity or are perceived as LGBTQI" (p. 1). Procedures cover: positive youth development; confidentiality; intake and classification; names and language; clothing and gender presentation; bathrooms and showers; medical and mental health care; searches; training of employees; youth education; and responding to harassment and discrimination.

"Lesbian, Gay, Bisexual, Transgender & Questioning." National Clearinghouse on Families & Youth. Accessed July 17, 2012. *http://ncfy.acf.hhs.gov/topics/lesbian-gay-bisexual-transgender-questioning*

"Lesbian, gay, bisexual, transgender and questioning youth often contend with obstacles that their heterosexual peers don't have to face: intolerant parents, judgmental peers, even physical threats. The Family and Youth Services Bureau emphasizes culturally competent and respectful care for youth regardless of sexual orientation and gender identity. NCFY's articles and resources can help youth-serving organizations understand and more effectively support lesbian, gay, bisexual, transgender, and questioning young people." [Publisher abstract]

"LGBT kids in the prison pipeline." The Public Intellectual. Accessed February 21, 2013. *http://thepublicintellectual.org/2011/05/02/lgbt-kids-in-the-school-to-prison-pipeline/*

> Angela Irvine, Associate Director at the National Council on Crime and Delinquency, discusses the disparities in detention and sentencing for LGBT youth, particularly those of color.

"LGBT Youth More Likely to Call Juvenile Prisons Home." Care2. Accessed February 26, 2013. *http://www.nccdglobal.org/news/lgbt-youth-more-likely-to-call-juvenile-prisons-home*

> This article summarizes the research from one chapter of the book, *Juvenile Justice: Advancing Research, Policy, and Practice.* Chapter 8 of this book focuses on LGBT youth in the juvenile justice system and their unique issues.

"LGBT Youth in Detention: Myth and Reality." New York Juvenile Justice Coalition. Accessed September 11, 2012. *http://nicic.gov/Library/026483*

> Ten myths regarding justice-involved lesbian, gay, bisexual, and transgender (LGBT) youth are addressed. The myths discussed are: adolescents are too youth to be aware of their sexual identity; LGBT youth are manipulative; LGBT youth should be less open about their sexuality in order not to get picked on; kids get picked on, so being LGBT should be no different; LGBT youth never complain so all must be OK; for their safety, LGBT youth should be separated from the general population; the only way to ensure LGBT youths' safety is to create separate facilities; since staff cannot address other youth with their nicknames, they should not use transgender youths' preferred names; transgender youth should not wear clothing according to their gender identity; and homosexuality should not be discussed in facilities because it will encourage such behavior.

"LGBTQ: Children, Youth & Families." NYC Administration for Children's Services. Accessed June 20, 2013. *http://www.nyc.gov/html/acs/html/lgbtq/lgbtq.shtml*

> This website was created to provide "an online portal that brings together in one easy-to-navigate location a wealth of LGBTQ resources, support, and guidance for young people, families, and professionals involved in child welfare and juvenile justice."

Loomis, Melissa, Jaime Yarussi, and Brenda Smith. "End Silence – Carlo's Question." The Project on Addressing Prison Rape. Washington, D.C. 2012. Accessed February 21, 2013. *http://www.wcl.american.edu/endsilence/documents/CarlosQuestionFINALJune2012.pdf*

> A graphic novel for "LGBTIQ youth, aged 14-18, that focuses on the various problems gender non-conforming youth face when under correctional supervision."

Majd, Katayoon, Jody Marksamer, and Carolyn Reyes. "Hidden Injustice: Lesbian, Gay, Bisexual, and Transgender Youth in Juvenile Courts". San Francisco: Legal Services for Children; Washington: National Juvenile Defender Center; San Francisco: National Center for Lesbian Rights, 2009. Accessed September 12, 2012. *http://www.equityproject.org/pdfs/hidden_injustice.pdf*

> This document "represents the first effort to examine the experiences of LGBT [Lesbian, Gay, Bisexual, and Transgender] youth in juvenile courts across the country" (p. 1). Ten chapters follow and executive summary: barriers to fair and effective juvenile justice systems; professionals' responsibility to treat youth in juvenile courts fairly; common misconceptions and biases about LGBT youth in the juvenile justice system; attempts to change, control, or punish LGBT adolescent sexual orientation and gender identity; impact of family rejection and school harassment on LGBT youth involvement in the juvenile justice system; lack of services to meet the needs of LGBT youth; harmful and inappropriate use of pretrial detention; unsafe and unfair conditions of confinement of LGBT youth; barrier to zealous defense advocacy for LGBT youth; and conclusion and recommendations. Appendixes include: glossary; redacted court order regarding transgender youth; and a model non-discriminatory services policy.

Marksamer, Jody. "And by the Way, Do You Know He Thinks He's a Girl? The Failures of Law, Policy, and Legal Representation for Transgender Youth in Juvenile Delinquency Courts." *Sexuality Research & Social Policy* 5, no. 1 (2008): 72-92. *http://www.equityproject.org/pdfs/and_by_the_way_article.pdf*

> Legal protections often denied transgender youth involved with the juvenile justice system are described. Sections contained in this article include: transgender youth are at risk for juvenile court intervention; overview of the juvenile delinquency system; the failures of juvenile court intervention for transgender youth; the failures of legal representation;

failure to provide appropriate treatment and rehabilitation plans; lack of access to counsel and the courts; lack of competence to work with transgender youth; lack of safety in juvenile correctional facilities; juvenile courts fail to uphold their responsibilities to protect the rights of transgender youth; broken promises, emotional trauma; fairness, dignity, and respect for transgender youth in juvenile courts; keeping transgender youth out of juvenile courts; protecting due-process rights of transgender youth in the courtroom; responding to unconstitutional conditions of confinement for transgender youth; and conclusion.

Marksamer, Jody, Dean Spade, and Gabriel Arkles. "A Place of Respect: A Guide for Group Care Facilities Serving Transgender and Gender Non-Conforming Youth." National Center for Lesbian Rights (NCLR). San Francisco, CA. Spring 2011. *http://www.nclrights.org/wp-content/uploads/2013/07/A_Place_Of_Respect.pdf*

"Transgender and gender non-conforming youth often face serious physical, emotional, and sexual abuse in group homes, detention centers, and correctional institutions. Because staff members are often unsure of how to provide respectful and supportive services to these youth, they may unwittingly subject them to situations that are discriminatory and harmful. This guide offers group care facilities information and tools to provide transgender and gender non-conforming young people with appropriate and informed care" (p. 2). Five chapters are contained in this publication: understanding transgender and gender non-conforming youth; the challenges of living with a stigmatized identity; group care facilities' legal responsibility to treat transgender and gender non-conforming youth fairly and keep them safe; best practices for working with transgender and gender non-conforming youth; and best practices for administrators for changing culture, adopting practice guidelines and policies, and training and evaluating staff.

Marksamer, Jody and Harper Jean Tobin. "Standing with LGBT Prisoners: An Advocate's Guide to Ending Abuse and Combating Imprisonment." Accessed April 2, 2014. *http://transequality.org/PDFs/JailPrisons_Resource_FINAL.pdf*

This toolkit is intended for advocates who would like to work, or are working, with local or state corrections or detention agencies to develop and implement more just and humane policies toward LGBT people. This could include statewide LGBT equality groups, state or local transgender organizations, legal advocacy groups, or groups of grassroots activists, as well as organizations already working on prison reform or criminal justice issues that want to incorporate the concerns of LGBT people in their work.

"Teen SENSE Model Policy: Staff Training Focusing on the Needs of Youth in State Custody, The Center for HIV Law and Policy (2012). Accessed January 20, 2015. *http://www.hivlawandpolicy.org/resources/model-policy-training-youth-facility-staff-ensuring-competence-includes-rights-and-needs*

> This is designed for use by agencies and jurisdictions that provide services for youth in out-of-home care, outlines the basic requirements for ensuring that staff in youth facilities are equipped to understand and protect the health and well-being of all youth, regardless of sexual orientation, gender identity, and gender expression. It serves as a companion to Teen SENSE Model Standards: Staff Training Focusing on the Needs of Youth in State Custody, which describes in detail the core components and educational objectives of appropriate staff training curricula. [Publisher abstract]

Perry, J.R. & Green, E.R. "Safe and Respected: Policy, Best Practices & Guidance for Serving Transgender & Gender Non-Conforming Children and Youth Involved in the Child Welfare, Detention, and Juvenile Justice Systems." New York City, NY: New York City's Administration for Children's Services. 2014. *http://www.nyc.gov/html/acs/downloads/pdf/lgbtq/FINAL_06_23_2014_WEB.pdf*

> This resource offers concrete guidance, strategies for successfully providing inclusive care, and resources that will enable child welfare and juvenile justice practitioners to meet the specific needs of TGNC children and young people.

"Promoting a Safe and Respectable Environment for Lesbian, Gay, Bisexual, Transgender and Questioning (LGBTQ) Youth and their Families Involved in the Child Welfare System; and Guidelines for Promoting a Safe and Respectable Environment for Lesbian, Gary, Bisexual, Transgender and Questioning (LGBTQ) Youth and their Families Involved with DYFJ." NYC Administration for Children's Services. July 27, 2011. *http://www.hunter.cuny.edu/socwork/nrcfcpp/info_services/download/ACS%20LGB TQ%20Policies.pdf*

> "The purpose of these policies is to provide direction to Children' Services and provider agency staff and volunteers on sensitive, inclusive and gender neutral practice as well as strategies to address bias and meet the unique needs of our youth and families."

"A Quick Guide for LGBTI Policy Development for Youth Confinement Facilities." Washington, D.C.: The Moss Group, Inc. and Washington, D.C.: National Institute of Corrections. November 2012. *https://s3.amazonaws.com/static.nicic.gov/Library/026701.pdf*

"This Quick Guide will help agencies and facilities develop a comprehensive response to working with lesbian, gay, bisexual, transgender and intersex (LGBTI) youth. It is not meant to provide an answer to every question or an in-depth discussion of all issues that agencies face or that the LGBTI population faces while in custody. It provides an overview of the important issues that agencies should consider when working to house and treat LGBTI youth in a way that is safe and consistent with an agency's mission, values, and security guidelines." This Quick Guide is organized chronologically according to the decisions an agency will have to make before and at the point when an LGBTI youth enters the system. These areas of focus include: Assessment of Agency Culture (as relates to LGBTI individuals); Assessment of Agency Staff and Administration Knowledge and Attitudes; Examination of Current Relevant Agency Norms; Development and Implementation Mechanisms; Development of Awareness of Current Legal Responsibilities; Foundational Issues; Intake Screening/Risk Assessment; Classification and Housing Placement; Medical and Mental Health Care; Information Management; Group Youth Management; Specific Safety and Privacy Concerns for Transgender and Intersex Youth; and Staff, Volunteer, and Contractor Training Requirements. (p. 1).

"Restoring Justice: A Blueprint for Ensuring Fairness, Safety, and Supportive Treatment of LGBT Youth in the Juvenile Justice System." Accessed January 26, 2015.
*http://nicic.gov/library/029686*

"Lesbian, gay, bisexual, and transgender, or LGBT, youth continue to be significantly over-represented in the nation's juvenile justice system, even as overall rates of youth incarceration are on the decline ... This brief [explains] what works for LGBT youth by outlining the critical components of model juvenile justice policies that are already being implemented around the country and offers sample language that all jurisdictions can adopt" (p. 1-2). Sections of this publication cover: LGBT youth experience high rates of discrimination and abuse; model policies exist and are working; nondiscrimination provisions—nondiscrimination and gender presentation; screening and intake; classification and housing placement—limits on isolation and segregation of LGBT youth, placement decisions based on gender identity, and classification decisions based on individualized assessment; confidentiality; privacy and safety of transgender youth; respectful communication-- no demeaning language, and preferred name and pronoun use; access to LGBT supports; medical and mental health services and treatment-- specific medical and mental health care needs of transgender youth, counseling should not try to change LGBT identity, sex-offender treatment, and provide appropriate medical and mental health care; staff training and policy dissemination; youth education and policy dissemination; and enforcement. "These policy guidelines reflect the best practices already in place around the country. All jurisdictions should adopt similar measures to ensure that LGBT youth under the supervision of the juvenile justice system are treated fairly, are free from harm, and receive the supportive treatment and services they deserve" (p. 13).

Ryan, Caitlin and Donna Futterman. Lesbian & Gay Youth. New York: Columbia University Press. 1998.

> This book is both a "resource, providing for the first time comprehensive guidelines for the care and counseling of lesbian, gay, bisexual, and transgendered youth, together with a compact review of the most recent information and research on lesbian and gay health and mental health, identity development and peer and family issues." p. xi

Society for Adolescent Health and Medicine. 2013. "Recommendations for Promoting the Health and Well-Being of Lesbian, Gay, Bisexual, and Transgender Adolescents: A Position Paper of the Society for Adolescent Health and Medicine." The Journal of Adolescent Health : Official Publication of the Society for Adolescent Medicine 52(4): 506-10.
*http://www.ncbi.nlm.nih.gov/pubmed/23521897*

> Adolescent health care providers frequently care for patients who identify as lesbian, gay, bisexual, or transgendered (LGBT), or who may be struggling with or questioning their sexual orientation or gender identity. Whereas these youth have the same health concerns as their non-LGBT peers, LGBT teens may face additional challenges because of the complexity of the coming-out process, as well as societal discrimination and bias against sexual and gender minorities. The Society for Adolescent Health and Medicine encourages adolescent providers and researchers to incorporate the impact of these developmental processes (and understand the impacts of concurrent potential discrimination) when caring for LGBT adolescents. The Society for Adolescent Health and Medicine also encourages providers to help positively influence policy related to LGBT adolescents in schools, the foster care system, and the juvenile justice system, and within the family structure. Consistent with other medical organizations, the Society for Adolescent Health and Medicine rejects the mistaken notion that LGBT orientations are mental disorders, and opposes the use of any type of reparative therapy for LGBT adolescents. [Journal abstract]

Substance Abuse and Mental Health Services Administration (SAHMSA) *Practitioner's Resource Guide: Helping Families to Support Their LGBT Children*, 2014.
*http://store.samhsa.gov//product/PEP14-LGBTKIDS*

This resource guide provides very important information for individuals helping families with lesbian, gay, bisexual, and transgender (LGBT) children involved with the juvenile justice system. Its intent is to help practitioners "understand the critical role of family acceptance and rejection in contributing to the health and well-being of adolescents who identify as lesbian, gay, bisexual and transgender ... [and] implement best practices in engaging and helping families and caregivers to support their LGBT children. The family intervention approach discussed in this guide is based on research findings and more than a decade of interactions and intervention work by the Family Acceptance Project (FAP) at San Francisco State University with very diverse families and their LGBT children" (p. 3). Sections address: the critical role of families in reducing risk and promoting well-being; helping families decrease rick and increase well-being for their LGBT children; increasing family support—how to help now; and resources for practitioners and families.

"Teen SENSE Model Policy: Staff Training Focusing on the Needs of Youth in State Custody, The Center for HIV Law and Policy (2012). Accessed January 20, 2015. *http://www.hivlawandpolicy.org/resources/model-policy-training-youth-facility-staff-ensuring-competence-includes-rights-and-needs.*

This is designed for use by agencies and jurisdictions that provide services for youth in out-of-home care, outlines the basic requirements for ensuring that staff in youth facilities are equipped to understand and protect the health and well-being of all youth, regardless of sexual orientation, gender identity, and gender expression. It serves as a companion to Teen SENSE Model Standards: Staff Training Focusing on the Needs of Youth in State Custody, which describes in detail the core components and educational objectives of appropriate staff training curricula. [Publisher abstract]

"The TREVOR Project". The Trevor Project. Accessed July 17, 2012. *http://www.thetrevorproject.org/*

This website (the TREVOR Project) is focused on providing crisis intervention and suicide prevention services to LGBTQ youth.

U.S. Bureau of Justice Statistics (Washington, DC). Sexual Victimization in Prisons and Jails Reported by Inmates, 2011–12, 2013. *http://www.bjs.gov/content/pub/pdf/svpjri1112.pdf*

This report presents statistics regarding the sexual victimization of prison and jail inmates by other inmates or staff. Sections of this publication cover:

highlights; National Inmate Survey; incidents of sexual victimizations; facility-level rates; demographic and other characteristics; special inmate populations—inmates ages 16 to 17; special inmate populations—inmates with mental health problems; and special inmate populations—inmates with a non-heterosexual sexual orientation. Some of the key findings include: 4% of prison inmates and 3.2% of jail inmates reported being sexually victimized; 1.8% of juveniles ages 16 to 17 reported being victimized by another inmate, with 3.2% reporting staff sexual misconduct; 6.3% of mentally ill inmates in prison reported sexual victimization by another inmate, with those in jails at 3.6%; and non-heterosexual inmates having the highest sexual victimization rates by another inmate of 12.2% in prison and 8.5% in jail, 5.4% and 4.3% respectively by staff.

"United States Reaches Agreement with Arcadia, California, School District to Resolve Sex Discrimination Allegations". July 24, 2013. *http://www.justice.gov/opa/pr/2013/July/13-crt-838.html*

> "The United States entered into a settlement agreement with the Arcadia Unified School District in Arcadia, Calif., to resolve an investigation into allegations of discrimination against a transgender student based on the student's sex. Under the agreement, approved by the district's school board unanimously last night, the school district will take a number of steps to ensure that the student, whose gender identity is male and who has consistently and uniformly presented as a boy at school and in all other aspects of his life for several years, will be treated like other male students while attending school in the district."

Valentino, Amanda. "Part 1: LGBTQ Youth in the Juvenile Justice System." American Bar Association. January 6, 2011. *http://apps.americanbar.org/litigation/committees/lgbt/articles/winter2011-valentino-juvenile-justice-system.html*

> This first of two articles highlights issues of LGBTQ youth in criminal justice, such as disproportionate representation, abuse and isolation.

Ware, Wesley. "Locked Up & Out: Lesbian, Gay, Bisexual, & Transgender Youth in Louisiana's Juvenile Justice System". New Orleans, LA: Juvenile Justice Project of Louisiana, 2010. Accessed September 12, 2012. *http://www.equityproject.org/pdfs/Locked-Up-Out.pdf*

> The strategies offered for addressing the challenges LGBT (lesbian, gay, bisexual, and transgender) youth must deal with in correctional facilities will provide guidance for other correctional agencies facing similar problems. Sections of this report include: introduction; LGBT 101; juvenile

justice in Louisiana; demographic profiles of Louisiana secure youth population; incarcerated youth in Louisiana; risk factors for LGBT youth in Louisiana; LGBT youth inside Louisiana's secure care facilities; recommendations for Louisiana and the Office of Juvenile Justice; conclusion; and resources for LGBT youth in Louisiana.

Wilber, Shannan, Caitlin Ryan, and Jody Marksamer. "CWLA Best Practices Guideline: Serving LGBT Youth in Out-of-Home Care". Washington: Child Welfare League of America, 2006. Accessed September 12, 2012. *http://www.nclrights.org/wp-content/uploads/2013/07/bestpracticeslgbtyouth.pdf*

> Guidance is provided for both child welfare and juvenile justice professionals who work with LGBT (lesbian, gay, bisexual, and transgender) youth in an out-of-home setting. The guidelines are based on best practices that are "grounded in a youth development approach that provides services and supports designed to promote young people's competencies and connect them to families and communities" (p. xiv). These guidelines are organized into the following areas: LGBT youth in out-of-home care; creating an inclusive organizational culture; a family-centered approach to serving LGBT youth; promoting positive adolescent development; collecting and managing confidential information; ensuring appropriate homes for LGBT youth; LGBT youth in institutional settings; and providing appropriate health, mental health, and education services for LGBT youth. A glossary is also included.

# Legal and Policy Considerations

"Advances in Juvenile Justice Reform: LGBTQ Youth in the System." National Juvenile Justice Network. Accessed March 17, 2014.
*http://www.njjn.org/our-work/juvenile-justice-reform-advances-lgbtq-youth-in-the-system*

> This webpage provides highlights policies created in New Orleans and New York City to protect LGBT youth in detention.

Cooper, Leslie. American Civil Liberties Union (ACLU), and National Center for Transgender Equality. *Protecting the Rights of Transgender Parents and Their Children: A Guide for Parents and Lawyers*, 2013.
*http://nicic.gov/Library/027557*

> "More and more transgender parents are fighting to protect their relationships with their children in the face of custody challenges. Yet they face significant obstacles. Parents who have come out or transitioned after having a child with a spouse or partner have seen their gender transition raised as a basis to deny or restrict child custody or visitation. Transgender people who formed families after coming out or transitioning have faced challenges to their legal status as parents, often based on attacks on the validity of their marriages ... The purpose of this guide is to provide information to transgender parents and their attorneys to help them protect parent-child relationships and assist them when faced with disputes over child custody issues" (p. 5). Sections of this report address: protecting against challenges to the parental fitness of transgender parents—overview of the case law, recommendations for parents prior to transitioning or coming out to their families, and advocacy suggestions for parents and their lawyers if faced with custody dispute; protecting against challenges to the legal parental status of transgender parents—the legal landscape, recommendations for parents to secure their status as legal parents, and advocacy suggestions for parents and their lawyers if faced with a challenge to legal parentage; and who to contact if facing a problem. Appendixes provide: an overview of case law regarding transgender parents; and sample expert testimony related to transgender issues.

"Andrea Fields, et al., Plaintiffs-Appellees, Cross-Appellants, v. Judy P. Smith, et al., Defendants-Appellants, Cross-Appellees. Appeals from the United States District Court for the Eastern District of Wisconsin". No. 2:06-cv-00112-CNC, August 5, 2011.
*http://nicic.gov/Library/025835*

The U.S. Appeals Court affirms the District Court's decision that Wisconsin's Act 105, the Inmate Sex Change Prevention Act, violates the Eighth Amendment's ban on cruel and unusual punishment. It should be noted that the plaintiffs had been receiving hormone treatment prior to the Acts passage.

Arkles, Gabriel. "Safety and Solidarity Across Gender Lines: Rethinking Segregation of Transgender People in Detention." *Temple Political & Civil Rights Law Review* 18, no. 2 (2009): 515-560.
*http://srlp.org/files/segregation_Arkles.pdf*

Transgender, intersex, and gender nonconforming (TIGNC) people, particularly people of color, are disproportionately incarcerated because of societal discrimination, widespread poverty, immigration policies, police profiling, and bias in court proceedings. Once incarcerated, TIGNC people, particularly transgender women placed in men's facilities, experience exceedingly high levels of sexual and other physical violence. Officials in detention systems often place TIGNC people against their will in isolating segregated settings as a form of protection, punishment, or prevention. At times advocates seem to assume that such placements are appropriate settings to protect TIGNC people from violence in detention. However, the premise that such placements are "protective" relies on at least two assumptions. The first is that isolation and control, rather than relationships and freedom, reduce violence. The second is that other prisoners, rather than facility staff, are the primary perpetrators of violence from whom TIGNC people need protection within detention systems. (Journal abstract)

Beyer, Dana and Jillian T. Weiss with Riki Wilchins. "New Title VII and EEOC Rulings Protect Transgender Employees." *Transgender Law Center.* 2014. Accessed January 21, 2015.
*http://transgenderlawcenter.org/wp-content/uploads/2014/01/TitleVII-Report-Final012414.pdf*

"EEOC—the federal agency in charge of enforcing employment discrimination laws—declared unanimously that anti-trans bias was sex discrimination under Title VII."

Cohen, Fred. "Transgender Prisoners' Right of Access to Medical Care in Prison." *Correctional Mental Health Report* 13, no. 4 (December 11, 2011): 49-63. *Criminal Justice Abstracts with Full Text, EBSCOhost* (accessed January 22, 2015).

This article discusses the overturning of Wisconsin law (Act 105) denying inmates diagnosed with Gender Identity Disorder (GID) medical care for hormonal therapy and sexual reassignment surgery. Also, includes references to additional GID case law.

Colopy, Travis Wright. "Setting Gender Identity Free: Expanding Treatment for Transsexual Inmates." Health Matrix 22 (2012)" 227-272.
*http://law.case.edu/journals/HealthMatrix/Documents/Colopy%20-%20Darby-SFP.pdf*

> The article is divided into four parts. "Part I will discuss general background information concerning what transsexualism is, the treatments prescribed by the medical community, and the significant problems transsexuals face in the United States. Part II will introduce the tax court case O'Donnabhain v. Commissioner and other indicia of the improving social, legal, and political situation for transsexuals. Part III will discuss Eighth Amendment protections for inmate health care, and case law demonstrating problems with current prison policies regarding care for transsexual inmates. Part IV will propose changes to prison policies so as to balance the respective constitutional rights and duties of inmates and officials."

"David H. Pickup, et al. v. Edmund G. Brown, Jr., Governor of the State of California in his official capacity, et al. United States Court of Appeals for the Ninth Circuit. No. 12-176981, April 17, 2013.
*http://cdn.ca9.uscourts.gov/datastore/opinions/2014/01/28/12-17681.pdf*

> Reversing an order granting preliminary injunctive relief in Welch v. Brown, 13-15023, and affirming the denial of preliminary injunctive relief in Pickup v. Brown, 12-17681, the panel held that California Senate Bill 1172, which bans state-licensed mental health providers from engaging in "sexual orientation change efforts" with patients under 18 years of age, does not violate the free speech rights of practitioners or minor patients, is neither vague nor overbroad, and does not violate parents' fundamental rights. The panel held that Senate Bill 1172 regulates professional conduct, not speech and therefore was subject only to a rational basis review.

Denver Sheriff Department. Office of the Director of Corrections/Undersheriff. "Transgender and Gender-Variant Inmates". Department Order 4005.1, Denver, CO, 2012.
*http://nicic.gov/Library/026337*

> This order provides guidelines that will "facilitate the elimination of discrimination against; and/or address the appropriate treatment of; and/or provide for the safety, security and medical needs of transgender and gender-variant inmates" (p. 1). Implementation and procedural guidelines

cover: intake and initial classification; searches; Blue Cards; medical staff notification; Transgender Review Board; long-term housing and classification; medical assessment and treatment; responsibility for training, management, and supervisors; and staff compliance. Appendixes include a copy of the "Statement if Search Preferences Form," "Blue Card," and "Transgender/Gender Variant Individual Genitalia Search Form."

Dolovich, Sharon. "Strategic Segregation in the Modern Prison." American Criminal Law Review 48, no. 1 (2011): 1-110.
*http://nicic.gov/library/026647*

> "In the Los Angeles County Jail—the biggest jail system in the country—officials have found a way to increase the personal security of gay men and trans women detainees without forcing them to choose between safety and community. For more than two decades, the L.A. County Sheriff's Department (the Department), which runs the County's jail system, has been systematically separating out the gay men and trans women admitted to the L.A. County Jail (the Jail) and housing them wholly apart from GP [general population]" (p. 3). This article is provides a great description of this segregated unit, designated as K6G, and is divided into four parts: prison rape, hypermasculinity, and the feminization of victims; the origins, mechanics, and effects of Los Angeles County's K6G Unit; K6G or not K6G—three critical perspectives—"demoralizing and dangerous"--the antisegregationist objection, drawing the line--the underinclusivity objection, and unconstitutional--the equal protection objection; and conclusion—the prospects for replication. "[G]ay men and trans women detained in the Jail [Unit K6G] are relatively free from the sexual harassment and forced or coerced sexual conduct that can be the daily lot of sexual minorities in other men's carceral facilities" (p. 3).

Duffy, Meredith. "Chapter 30: Special Information for Lesbian, Gay, Bisexual, and Transgender Prisoners, in A Jailhouse Lawyer's Manual". *Columbia Human Rights Law Review*, 2009. Accessed September 12, 2012.
*http://www3.law.columbia.edu/hrlr/JLM/Chapter_30.pdf*

> Individuals needing basic legal information for federal and New York prisons can find it in this publication. Sections of this chapter are: introduction; changes in the law; unequal treatment because of sexual orientation or gender identity; your right to control your gender presentation while in prison; your right to confidentiality regarding your sexual orientation or gender identity; assault and harassment; housing and protective custody; visitation rights—special issues for LGBT (lesbian, gay, bisexual, and transgender) prisoners; right to receive LGBT literature; and conclusion.

"Federal appeals court reinstates prisoner's sex-change lawsuit." Reuters. January 28, 2013.
*http://www.reuters.com/article/2013/01/29/us-usa-crime-sexchange-idUSBRE90S03X20130129*

> "The 4th U.S. Circuit Court of Appeals found that Ophelia Azriel De'lonta, born Michael Stokes, can argue that denying her the surgery violates the Eighth Amendment's prohibition against cruel and unusual punishment."

The Fenway Institute. "The National LGBT Health Education Center." Accessed January 14, 2015.
*http://www.lgbthealtheducation.org/*

> The National LGBT Health Education Center provides educational programs, resources, and consultation to health care organizations with the goal of optimizing quality, cost-effective health care for lesbian, gay, bisexual, and transgender (LGBT) people.

> The Education Center is a part of The Fenway Institute, the research, training, and health policy division of Fenway Health, a Federally Qualified Health Center, and one of the world's largest LGBT-focused health centers. [Publisher abstract]

Gruberg, Sharita. "Dignity Denied: LGBT Immigrants in U.S. Immigration Detention." Center for American Progress. November 2013.
*http://nicic.gov/library/028213*

> "This report will examine the mistreatment LGBT immigrants face in immigration detention; the steps that Immigration and Customs Enforcement, or ICE, has taken in an attempt to address these issues; the impact that legislation pending before Congress would have on immigration enforcement; and recommendations for how to ensure enforcement of immigration laws is conducted in a manner that is effective and humane."

Harris County Sheriff's Office (HCSO) (Houston, TX). *Lesbian, Gay, Bisexual, Transgender and Intersex, (L.G.B.T.I.)*, 2013.
*http://nicic.gov/Library/027721*

> "This Order provides guidelines for the Harris County Sheriff's Office (HCSO) to follow in order to meet federal statutes and regulations, American Correctional Association (ACA) Standards, National Commission on

Correctional Health Care (NCCHC) standards, Prison Rape Elimination Act (PREA), and other Texas standards, statutes, regulations, guidelines, directives, or requirements that: A. Facilitate the elimination of discrimination against; and B. Address the appropriate classification, housing and treatment of; and C. Provide for the specific safety, security and medical needs of Lesbian, Gay, Bisexual, Transgender, and Intersex (LGBTI) inmates in a humane and respectful manner while maintaining the safety, security and good order of all HCSO facilities; and D. Establish sanctions for any violation of this policy" (p. 1). Procedures cover: employee conduct, notification, identification, searches, intake screening, Gender Classification Committee, reassessment, complaints and grievances, inmate services, use of screening information and confidentiality, LGBTI Liaison(s); and employee training (training content and refresher training).

Idaho Department of Corrections. "Gender Identity Disorder: Healthcare for Offenders with". Version 3.2. Control Number: 401.06.03.501, Boise, ID, 2011. *http://www.idoc.idaho.gov/content/policy/562*

The purpose of this standard operating procedure (SOP) is to establish guidelines for the diagnosis, treatment, management, and placement of offenders diagnosed with gender identity disorder (GID) to ensure offender safety and access to appropriate and necessary medical and mental health treatment. This SOP defines the extent and general limits of healthcare services provided to offenders identified as meeting the criteria for diagnosis of GID as outlined within the most current Diagnostic and Statistical Manual of Mental Disorders (DSM)" (p. 3). General requirements cover: initial reporting; referral and placement of the offender; evaluation of the offender; evaluator findings, diagnosis, and reporting; Chief Psychologist's review of findings; Management and Treatment Committee (MTC) meeting; Administrative Review Committee (ARC) meeting; final approval of the Management and Placement Plan; implementation of this plan; moral and ethical treatment of offenders diagnosed with GID; and subsequent reviews and evaluations for GID.

*Identification, Treatment and Correctional Management of Inmates Diagnosed with Gender Identity Disorder (GID).* Milford, MA: Massachusetts Dept. of Corrections. 2012.
*http://nicic.gov/Library/026740*

"The purpose of this policy is to establish guidelines for the identification, treatment, and institutional management of inmates diagnosed with Gender Identity Disorder (GID)" (p. 1). Procedures cover: responsibilities of the GID clinical supervision group; responsibilities of the GID Treatment Committee; identification and diagnosis of inmates with GID; treatment planning for inmates with GID; reporting; security review; and management and placement. A sample "Gender Identity (GID) Mental Health Referral" is also included.

"Interactions with Transgender, Intersex, and Gender Nonconforming (TIGN) Individuals." General Order G02-01-03. Chicago Police Department. Last modified August 21, 2012. *http://directives.chicagopolice.org/directives/data/a7a57b38-1394a4ae-75313-94a4-b606a68cfab99615.html?hl=true*

This Chicago Police Department general order establishes policies for interactions with TIGN individuals regarding their safety. It also defines terms pertaining to processing and establishes procedures for processing TIGN individuals. "

"LAPD Drops Transgender Pat-Downs, Eyes Separate Detention Space". Los Angeles CBS Local. Last modified April 13, 2012. *http://losangeles.cbslocal.com/2012/04/13/lapd-drops-transgender-pat-downs-eyes-separate-detention-space/*

This news article, from April 2012, highlights the changes in LAPD policy in regards to treatment and facilities for transgender people.

"LGBT Rights: Lesbian Gay Bisexual & Transgender Project". American Civil Liberties Union. Accessed September 12, 2012. *http://www.aclu.org/lgbt-rights*

The LGBT Project works for an America free of discrimination based on sexual orientation and gender identity. This means an America where LGBT people can live openly, where our identities, relationships and families are respected, and where there is fair treatment on the job, in schools, housing, public places, health care, and government programs. (Abstract from website)

Marksamer, Jody, and National Institute of Corrections (Washington, DC). *Excerpts from LGBT and TG Policies by Faculties and Departments: Organized by Topic*, 2012.

Excerpts are organized according to: non-discrimination provisions—TG (transgender) inmates, LGBT inmates, and LGBT youth; intake screening—TG arrestees and inmates; classification and housing/placement—classification decisions for LGBTQ youth based on an individualized assessment, limits on isolation and segregation of LGBT youth, LGBT youth not treated as sex offenders, LGBT youth and roommates, TG housing assessment with TG Committee, limitation on the use of isolation and access to services for TG inmates, no blanket housing policies for TG individuals, TG girls in girls units, and decision making committee for LGBTQ youth housing and clothing; specific privacy and safety concerns for transgender and intersex inmates/youth—showering, restroom practices that protect inmate from abuse by other inmates, and searches of arrestees, inmates, or juveniles; inmate/youth management—clothing and grooming, and access to LGBT supportive materials and programs; respectful communication with LGBTI inmates/youth—no demeaning language directed to youth or adults, and names and pronoun use; privacy and confidentiality—LGBT youth; medical/mental health services/treatment—specific medical and mental health care needs of transgender inmates/youth, and counseling should not try to change LGBTI identity; staff/volunteer/contractor tracking requirements— juvenile and adult facilities; and inmate/youth education.

"Michelle Kosilek, Plaintiff, Appellee, v. LUIS S. SPENCER, Commissioner of the Massachusetts Department of Correction, Defendant, Appellant. Appeal from the United States District Court for the District of Massachusetts." December 16, 2014. *http://media.ca1.uscourts.gov/pdf.opinions/12-2194P2-01A.pdf*

This case involves important issues that arise under the Eighth Amendment to the U.S. Constitution. We are asked to determine whether the district court erred in concluding that the Massachusetts Department of Correction ("DOC") has violated the Cruel and Unusual Punishment Clause of the Eighth Amendment by providing allegedly inadequate medical care to prisoner Michelle Kosilek ("Kosilek"). More precisely, we are faced with the question whether the DOC's choice of a particular medical treatment is constitutionally inadequate, such that the district court acts within its power to issue an injunction requiring provision of an alternative treatment-a treatment which would give rise to new concerns related to safety and prison security.

After carefully considering the community standard of medical care, the adequacy of the provided treatment, and the valid security concerns articulated by the DOC, we conclude that the district court erred and that the care provided to Kosilek by the DOC does not violate the Eighth Amendment. We therefore reverse the district court's grant of injunctive relief, and we remand with instructions to dismiss the case.

Millett, Gregorio A., John L. Peterson, Richard J. Wolitski, and Ron Stall. "Greater Risk for HIV Infection of Black Men Who Have Sex With Men: A Critical Literature Review." *American Journal of Public Health* 96, no. 6 (June 2006): 1007–19. *http://www.ncbi.nlm.nih.gov/pmc/articles/PMC1470628/*

HIV rates are disproportionately higher for Black men who have sex with men (MSM) than for other MSM. We reviewed the literature to examine 12 hypotheses that might explain this disparity.

We found that high rates of HIV infection for Black MSM were partly attributable to a high prevalence of sexually transmitted diseases that facilitate HIV transmission and to undetected or late diagnosis of HIV infection; they were not attributable to a higher frequency of risky sexual behavior, non-gay identity, or sexual nondisclosure, or to reported use of alcohol or illicit substances. Evidence was insufficient to evaluate the remaining hypotheses.

Future studies must address these hypotheses to provide additional explanations for the greater prevalence of HIV infection among Black MSM. [Publication abstract]

Neil, Martha. "Federal Judge Strikes State-Law Ban on Hormone Treatment for Transgendered Inmates". ABA Journal News. Accessed July 30, 2012. *http://www.abajournal.com/news/article/federal_judge_strikes_state_law_that_bans_treatment_for_transgendered_inmat/*

This news article reports on the unconstitutionality of a state law in Wisconsin, which banned transgender inmates from receiving hormone therapy.

"Patti Hammon Shaw, Plaintiff, v. District of Columbia, et.al." Memorandum Opinion. Civil Action No. 11-0946 (ESH). November 18, 2011. *http://www.courthousenews.com/2011/11/22/Patti%20Hammond%20Shaw%20order.pdf*

A District of Columbia district court opinion regarding the treatment of Pattie Hammond Shaw, a transgendered female, upon her arrest and while she was detained. Eighth Amendment claims were granted in part and denied in part.

Philadelphia Police Department. "Department Interactions with Transgender Individuals". Directive 152, December 20, 2013. *http://matchbin-assets.s3.amazonaws.com/public/sites/357/assets/55XE_Directive152.pdf*

This directive establishes policies for interactions with transgender individuals to provide for the safety of police officers and citizens, and for the protection of the constitutional rights of citizens in all official interactions.

"Police, Transgender Groups Building Trust." Timesunion.com. Accessed February 27, 2013.
*http://www.timesunion.com/local/article/Police-transgender-groups-building-trust-4142592.php*

> This article discusses how Albany's law enforcement officials are working to rewrite protocol and procedures, as well as create new police training, with transgender community input.

"Policy Recommendations Regarding LGBT People in California Prisons". Transgender Law Center. Accessed September 12, 2012.
*http://www.transgenderlawcenter.org/issues/prisons/policy-recommendations-regarding-lgbt-people-in-california-prisons*

> Effective practices for ensuring the rights of LGBT (lesbian, gay, bisexual, and transgender) inmates are explained. Strategies for protecting LGBT prisoners are organized according to: classification; harassment, abuse, and sexual assault; health care; and reentry.

"Preventing the Sexual Abuse of Lesbian, Gay, Bisexual, Transgender, and Intersex People in Correctional Settings". Washington: National Center for Transgender Equality; San Francisco: National Center for Lesbian Rights; New York: American Civil Liberties Union; San Francisco: Transgender Law Center; New York: Lambda Legal. Last modified May 10, 2010.
*http://www.wcl.american.edu/endsilence/documents/ACLULambdaNCLRNCTETLC CommentsonPREAStandards.pdf*

> The "need for all four sets of standards [found in the National Standards to Prevent, Detect, and Respond to Prison Rape] to account for the vulnerabilities of LGBTI [lesbian, gay, bisexual, transgender, and intersex] individuals in detention" is explained (p. 2). Sections of these comments include: LGBTI people in detention are particularly at risk of sexual abuse; support for specific standards; recommendations to enhance the standards; responses to questions in the ANPR (Advance Notice of Proposed Rulemaking); and conclusion.

"A Quick Guide for LGBTI Policy Development for Adult Prisons and Jails." Washington, D.C.: The Moss Group, Inc. and Washington, D.C.: National Institute of Corrections. November 2012.
*http://nicic.gov/Library/026702*

> "This Quick Guide will help agencies and facilities develop a comprehensive

response to working with lesbian, gay, bisexual, transgender and intersex (LGBTI) inmates. It is not meant to provide an answer to every question or an in-depth discussion of all issues that agencies face or that the LGBTI population faces while in custody. It provides an overview of the important issues that agencies should consider when working to house and treat LGBTI inmates in a way that is safe and consistent with an agency's mission, values, and security guidelines." This Quick Guide is organized chronologically according to the decisions an agency will have to make before and at the point when an LGBTI individual enters the system. These areas of focus include: Assessment of Agency Culture (as relates to LGBTI individuals); Assessment of Agency Staff and Administration Knowledge and Attitudes; Examination of Current Relevant Agency Norms; Development and Implementation Mechanisms; Development of Awareness of Current Legal Responsibilities; Foundational Issues; Intake Screening/Risk Assessment; Classification and Housing Placement; Medical and Mental Health Care; Information Management; Group Inmate Management; Specific Safety and Privacy Concerns for Transgender and Intersex Inmates; and Staff, Volunteer, and Contractor Training Requirements. (p. 1).

Scheel, Murray D. and Claire Eustace. "Model Protocols on the Treatment of Transgender Persons by San Francisco County Jail". National Lawyers Guild & City & County of San Francisco Human Rights Commission. Last modified August 7, 2002.
*http://www.transgenderlaw.org/resources/sfprisonguidelines.doc*

This article contains "model protocols for the treatment of transgender people by San Francisco County jail personnel. These protocols will help jail staff prevent discrimination against transgender inmates by articulating rules that are both respectful of transgender inmates' needs and administrable. The protocols will also bring San Francisco County Jail into compliance with local anti-discrimination laws. These protocols are to be used by jail staff as a supplement to the existing jail protocols in order to protect the rights of transgender inmates." (From introduction)

Shah, Benish A. "Lost in the Gender Maze: Placement of Transgender Inmates in the Prison System". *Journal of Race, Gender and Ethnicity* 5, no. 1 (2010): 39-56.
*http://www.tourolaw.edu/JournalRGE/uploads/Issues/Vol5Issue1/Shah_Final.pdf*

This article addresses one critical issue, of the many, faced by transgender inmates: placement into male or female prisons and holding cells based on genitalia instead of gender identification. Part I will address the definition of transgender under the legal system. Part II reviews the abuse suffered by transgender individuals from the humiliation in the initial booking process to the sexual assaults suffered repeatedly in prisons, based upon genitalia based prison placement. Part III analyzes the possible solutions to the placement problem, including self-identification based placement, administrative segregation, and Category B prisons. Part IV provides a few proposed solutions to provide relatively "quick" relief to transgender inmates while larger policy issues are battled out in this progressive society. (Abstract from author)

"Transgender woman settles suit with Cicero, attorneys say." Chicago Tribune. Last modified August 7, 2012. *http://www.chicagotribune.com/news/local/breaking/chi-transgender-woman-settles-suit-with-cicero-attorneys-say-20120807,0,6321213.story*

> "A transgender woman who said Cicero police officers harassed and humiliated her has settled a lawsuit for $10,000 along with a pledge that the town will adopt a policy for dealing respectfully with transgender people, her attorneys said Tuesday (August 7, 2012)."

"Treatment of Transgender Persons [and] Procedure." *Volume 4: Medical Services.* Sacramento, CA: Correctional Health Care Services, 2012. Accessed January 21, 2015.
*http://www.cphcs.ca.gov/docs/imspp/IMSPP-v04-ch26.2.pdf*
> "The purpose of this policy is to state the generally accepted standards for diagnosis and treatment of GID [gender identity disorder] patient-inmates in a correctional setting. Additionally, this policy shall include the factors that must be considered by primary care providers (PCP) as they exercise their clinical judgment while providing constitutionally adequate medical care and personal safety to patient-inmates who have been diagnosed with GID" (p. 1). Procedures of 4.26.1 covering the treatment for GID patient-inmates are: required mental health evaluation; required medical history and physical/specialty consult; creation and implementation of a treatment plan; informed consent required prior to treatment; patient-inmates entering correctional facilities on hormone therapy; and patient-inmates not on hormone therapy upon entry into correctional facilities, but who later self-identify as GID. Procedures covered by 4.26.2 are: diagnostic procedure; hormonal therapy for transgender adults; adverse outcome prevention and long-term care; housing; clothing for male-to-female transgendered patient-inmates who are housed at male institutions; and clothing for female-to-male transgendered patient-inmates who are housed at female institutions.

"Tribal Equity Toolkit: Tribal Resolutions and Codes to Support Two Spirit & LGBT Justice in Indian Country." Portland, OR: Legal Aid Services of Oregon, Native

American Program, Lewis & Clark College, and Western States Center. 2012.
*http://nicic.gov/Library/026630*

> "Two Spirit is a term in the English Language that attempts to incorporate and honor the hundreds of ancient, respectful, Native Language terms that were used for thousands of years within our Tribal societies. Two-Spirit is used to denote people who have special roles within our communities, our cultures, and our ceremonial life (p. 3) ... This guide is intended to give tribal legislators a brief overview of legal issues that impact the equal treatment of Two Spirit or lesbian, gay, bisexual, and transgender (LGBT) individuals. The Guide identifies areas in which existing laws may discriminate against LGBT individuals, and provides sample resolution and code language for tribal lawmakers to consider adopting to maximize LGBT equality within their communities.

"United States of America v. City of New Orleans". United States District Court for the Eastern District of Louisiana. Case 2:12-cv-01924-SM-JCW, January 11, 2013.
*http://www.justice.gov/crt/about/spl/documents/nopd_agreement_1-11-13.pdf*

> This agreement and the provisions listed are the result of a May 2010 investigation of the New Orleans Police Department by the United States Department of Justice for "an alleged pattern or practice of unlawful misconduct". Section VIII focuses on Bias-Fee Policing and section IX on Policing Free of Gender Bias".

The United States Department of Justice. Office on Violence Against Women (OVW). "VAWA 2013 Nondiscrimination Provision: Making Programs Accessible to All Victims of Domestic Violence, Sexual Assault, Dating Violence, and Stalking." April 9, 2014. Accessed January 14, 2015.
*http://www.justice.gov/ovw/blog/vawa-2013-nondiscrimination-provision-making-programs-accessible-all-victims-domestic*

> This groundbreaking provision will ensure that lesbian, gay, bisexual and transgender  (LGBT) victims of domestic violence, sexual assault, dating violence and stalking are not denied, on the basis of sexual orientation or gender identity, access to the critical services that OVW supports. [Publisher abstract]

"Vanessa Adams, legal name, Nicholas Adams, Plaintiff, v. Federal Bureau of Prisons, et al., Defendants". United States District Court, District of Massachusetts. Civil Action No. 09-10272-JLT, June 7, 2010.
*http://nicic.gov/Library/025834*

"Plaintiff, an inmate in the custody of the Federal Bureau of Prisons, asserts that Defendants have subjected her to cruel and unusual punishment in violation of the Eighth Amendment to the United States Constitution by denying her appropriate medical treatment for her diagnosed condition of Gender Identity Disorder. Presently at issue is Defendants' Motion to Dismiss the Amended Complaint [#20]. For the following reasons, Defendants' Motion to Dismiss the Amended Complaint [#20] is DENIED" (p. 1).

Western New England University School of Law (Springfield, MA). *Gender & Sexuality in the ABA Standards on the Treatment of Prisoners*, 2012. *http://nicic.gov/Library/027269*

Anyone involved in inmate management should be aware of this issues addressed by these standards, especially in light of PREA (Prison Rape Elimination Act). "This Article describes provisions of the recently promulgated American Bar Association Criminal Justice Standards on the Treatment of Prisoners (2010 Standards or Standards) that address issues of gender and sexuality in a correctional setting" (p. 1217-1218). This paper is divided into four parts. Part I. Development of the ABA Standards on the Treatment of Prisoners—the road to revision. Part II. Updated provisions affecting women prisoners: screening and classification; pregnancy and childbirth; and co-corrections and equal protection. Part III. New provisions addressing sexual abuse, privacy and LGBT prisoners: custodial sexual abuse and prison sexual violence; searches and cross-gender supervision; lesbian, gay, and bisexual prisoners; and provisions affecting transgender prisoners. Part IV. Conclusion.

Woods, Jordan Blair, et al. "Interactions of Transgender Latina Women with Law Enforcement." *Policing : A Journal of Policy and Practice* 7.4 (Dec 2013): 379. Accessed January 21, 2015. *http://williamsinstitute.law.ucla.edu/wp-content/uploads/Galvan-Bazargan-Interactions-April-2012.pdf*

To date, very few researchers have explored transgender women's interactions with law enforcement agencies and officers. Addressing this research gap, this study examines the interactions of Latina transgender women with law enforcement. The investigators conducted semi-structured interviews of 220 low-income Latina transgender women recruited from a variety of community-based organizations and sources across Los Angeles County, California. The findings lend support to the conclusion that transgender women, and especially transgender women of colour, are common victims of verbal harassment, physical assault, and sexual assault perpetrated by law enforcement officers. The findings also lend support to the propositions that many transgender women perceive their personal interactions with law enforcement officers negatively, and view reports of crime against them as mishandled or ignored. The findings are discussed in light of the implications for law enforcement's interactions with transgender women and transgender communities of colour in particular. [Publication abstract]

# Medical and Mental Health

"2011 Operations Manual ICE Performance-Based National Detention Standards (PBNDS)". U.S. Department of Homeland Security. Immigration and Customs Enforcement (ICE). Accessed September 11, 2012. *http://www.ice.gov/detention-standards/2011/*

> Section 4.3 of the 2011 revision of ICE Detention Standards addresses the area of Medical Care. The standards make specific reference to the care and treatment of transgender detainees.

"Answers to Your Questions about Transgender People, Gender Identity, and Gender Expression." Washington: D.C. American Psychological Association (APA): APA Lesbian, Gay, Bisexual, and Transgender Concerns Office and APA Public and Member Communications, 2011. Last updated 2014. *http://www.apa.org/topics/lgbt/transgender.pdf*

> This brochure provides general information about transgender health, advocacy, and human rights.

"Being transgender no longer a 'mental disorder': APA." NBCNEWS.com. Last updated September 13, 2013. *http://www.msnbc.com/melissa-harris-perry/being-transgender-no-longer-mental-disorde*

> The fifth edition of the *Diagnostic and Statistical Manual of Mental Disorders* has removed being transgender as a mental disorder. "Transgender people will now be diagnosed with 'gender dysphoria,' which means emotional stress related to gender identity. 'Gender identity disorder' had been listed as a mental disorder since the third edition of the DSM more than 20 years ago."

Brewer, R.A., Magnus, M., Kuo, I., Wang, L., Liu, T.Y. et al.. Exploring the relationship between incarceration and HIV among black men who have sex with men in the United States. *Journal of Acquired Immune Deficiency Syndromes*, 65, no. 2, (2014): 218-225. *http://hsrc.himmelfarb.gwu.edu/sphhs_epibiostats_facpubs/110/*

> This study examined the predictors of new incarceration and their association with HIV infection among 1278 black men who have sex with men enrolled and followed up in the HIV Prevention Trials Network 061

study. HIV Prevention Trials Network 061 was conducted to determine the feasibility and acceptability of a multicomponent intervention to reduce HIV infection among BMSM in 6 US cities. In this study, multivariable logistic regression models were used to explore the association between incarceration during study follow-up and several demographic, behavioral, and psychosocial variables at baseline found to be significant in bivariate analyses. In addition, Cox proportional hazard regression was used to explore the association between incarceration during study follow-up and incident HIV infection. Among the 1278 BMSM with follow-up data, 305 (24%) reported a new incarceration within 1 year of entering the study with an estimated incarceration incidence of 35% (95% confidence interval: 31% to 38%). After adjusting for confounders, lower education, lower annual income, previous incarceration frequency, and higher levels of perceived racism were significantly associated with new incarcerations during study follow-up. There was no observed association between incarceration during study follow-up and incident HIV infection. The very high level of new incarcerations highlights the importance of structural-level interventions to prevent incarceration among economically disenfranchised black men who have sex with men in the United States. [Journal abstract]

Brown, George R. "Autocastration and Autopenectomy as Surgical Self-Treatment in Incarcerated Persons with Gender Identity Disorder." *International Journal of Transgenderism*, 12, no. 1 (May 7, 2010): 31-39.

The author reports on a case series of four inmates who engaged in attempted or completed surgical self-treatment of their gender dysphoria via autocastration, autopenectomy, or a combination in the absence of concomitant psychosis, intoxication, or other comorbidities that could reasonably account for this rare behavior. These behaviors occurred in the context of persistent denials of access to transgender health care in prison settings. The literature on genital self-harm is also reviewed. Incarcerated persons with severe GID may resort to life-threatening surgical self-treatments when persistently denied access to psychiatric evaluation and cross-sex hormonal treatment. In all cases of surgical self-treatment (SST; i.e., autocastration with the primary intent to reduce circulating testosterone levels) the intensity of gender dysphoria decreased compared to reported baseline levels, although symptoms of GID were still present. Of the four inmates, two were able to obtain access to cross-sex hormones after successful litigation at the time of this writing; another was not. One case remains active. This case series expands the limited literature on surgical self-treatment in the form of autocastration and autopenectomy with a focus on the potential influence of incarceration with denial of access to transgender health care. [Journal abstract]

Brown, George R., and Everett McDuffie. "Health Care Policies Addressing Transgender Inmates in Prison Systems in the United States." *Journal of Correctional Health Care*, v. 15 n. 4, 2009.

> "The purpose of this study is to present the current situation regarding access to health care for inmates with GID [gender identity disorders] and the related issue of housing in a single reference source available to those who are faced with this issue as health care providers in corrections setting' (p. 282). Results explained cover policies and directives, and transsexual management and treatment committees. A table is included that supplies a summary of policies and directives that address the health care management of transgender inmates. While some agencies allow access to cross-sex hormones, most deny any surgery to treat GID. [Journal abstract]

Brown, George R. 2009. "Recommended Revisions to the World Professional Association for Transgender Health's Standards of Care Section on Medical Care for Incarcerated Persons with Gender Identity Disorder." *International Journal of Transgenderism* 11 (2): 133–39.

> The introduction of comments regarding the care of persons with gender identity disorder (GID) residing in prison settings began in 1998 with Version 5 of the Standards of Care (SOC), the first major revision of the SOC since 1985. Minor revisions to this brief section were made for Version 6 in 2001. Since 2001, there have been many legal and regulatory actions in countries where the SOC are widely used as the minimum standards to evaluate and treat persons with GID that have referenced this section in the SOC. The original paragraph addressing care for incarcerated persons has proven to be helpful by its existence, but limiting in its brevity and lack of scope. Version 7, likely to be a significant revision compared with the minor changes in Version 6, can be informed by the information that has come to light in the last 6 years, most notably through court actions that have used, or misused, the SOC. This invited article reviews the background of this section, rationale for revisions, suggested conceptual changes, and specific content for consideration for inclusion in Version 7 of the SOC.

Byne, William, et. al. "Report of the American Psychiatric Association Task Force on Treatment of Gender Identity Disorder". *Archives of Sexual Behavior* 41, no. 4 (2012): 759-796. Accessed on September 4, 2012. *http://www.apa.org/pi/lgbt/resources/policy/gender-identity-report.pdf*

> Both the diagnosis and treatment of Gender Identity Disorder (GID) are controversial. Although linked, they are separate issues and the DSM does not evaluate treatments. The Board of Trustees (BOT) of the American Psychiatric Association (APA), therefore, formed a Task Force charged to perform a critical review of the literature on the treatment of GID at different ages, to assess the quality of evidence pertaining to treatment, and

to prepare a report that included an opinion as to whether or not sufficient credible literature exists for development of treatment recommendations by the APA. The literature on treatment of gender dysphoria in individuals with disorders of sex development was also assessed. The completed report was accepted by the BOT on September 11, 2011. The quality of evidence pertaining to most aspects of treatment in all subgroups was determined to be low; however, areas of broad clinical consensus were identified and were deemed sufficient to support recommendations for treatment in all subgroups. With subjective improvement as the primary outcome measure, current evidence was judged sufficient to support recommendations for adults in the form of an evidence-based APA Practice Guideline with gaps in the empirical data supplemented by clinical consensus. The report recommends that the APA take steps beyond drafting treatment recommendations. These include issuing position statements to clarify the APA's position regarding the medical necessity of treatments for GID, the ethical bounds of treatments of gender variant minors, and the rights of persons of any age who are gender variant, transgender or transsexual. (Journal abstract)

Catz, Sheryl, et. al. "Prevention Needs of HIV-Positive Men and Women Awaiting Release from Prison". *AIDS and Behavior* 16, no. 1 (2012): 108-120. Accessed September 11, 2012.
*http://www.ncbi.nlm.nih.gov/pmc/articles/PMC3428225/*

Greater understanding of barriers to risk reduction among incarcerated HIV+ persons reentering the community is needed to inform culturally tailored interventions. This qualitative study elicited HIV prevention-related information, motivation and behavioral skills (IMB) needs of 30 incarcerated HIV+ men and women awaiting release from state prison. Unmet information needs included risk questions about viral loads, positive sexual partners, and transmission through casual contact. Social motivational barriers to risk reduction included partner perceptions that prison release increases sexual desirability, partners' negative condom attitudes, and HIV disclosure-related fears of rejection. Personal motivational barriers included depression and strong desires for sex or substance use upon release. Behavioral skills needs included initiating safer behaviors with partners with whom condoms had not been used prior to incarceration, disclosing HIV status, and acquiring clean needles or condoms upon release. Stigma and privacy concerns were prominent prison context barriers to delivering HIV prevention services during incarceration. [Journal abstract]

"Committing to Safety and Respect for LGBTI Youth and Adults in Confinement: Lessons from Two Agencies." National PREA Resource Center. Accessed January 16, 2015.

*http://www.prearesourcecenter.org/node/2868*

> Research has shown that lesbian, gay, bisexual, and transgender (LGBT) people face a higher risk of sexual victimization in confinement. Recent Bureau of Justice Statistics surveys found that adults and youth in confinement who identify as lesbian, gay, or bisexual were much more likely to have experienced sexual victimization by another inmate than their heterosexual counterparts. [Publisher abstract]

"Gender Dysphoria". American Psychiatric Association. Accessed August 6, 2013. *http://www.dsm5.org/Documents/Gender%20Dysphoria%20Fact%20Sheet.pdf*

> This fact sheet on Gender Dysphoria provides a brief definition of the disorder, guidelines for care, characteristics of the condition, and discussion of the stigma around the disorder.

Haas, Ann, Philip Rodgers and Jody Herman. The "Suicide Attempts among Transgender and Gender Non-Conforming Adults: Findings of the National Transgender Discrimination Survey." January 2014. *http://williamsinstitute.law.ucla.edu/wp-content/uploads/AFSP-Williams-Suicide-Report-Final.pdf*

> The prevalence of suicide attempts among respondents to the National Transgender Discrimination Survey (NTDS), conducted by the National Gay and Lesbian Task Force and National Center for Transgender Equality, is 41 percent, which vastly exceeds the 4.6 percent of the overall U.S. population who report a lifetime suicide attempt, and is also higher than the 10-20 percent of lesbian, gay and bisexual adults who report ever attempting suicide. In the present study, we sought to increase understanding of suicidal behavior among transgender and gender non-conforming people through an in-depth analysis of NTDS data.

"The Health of Lesbian, Gay, Bisexual, and Transgender People: Building a Foundation for Better Understanding - Institute of Medicine." Accessed March 17, 2014. *http://www.iom.edu/Reports/2011/The-Health-of-Lesbian-Gay-Bisexual-and-Transgender-People.aspx*

> To help assess the state of the science, the National Institutes of Health (NIH) asked the IOM to evaluate current knowledge of the health status of lesbian, gay, bisexual, and transgender populations; to identify research gaps and opportunities; and to outline a research agenda to help NIH focus its

research in this area. The IOM finds that to advance understanding of the health needs of all LGBT individuals, researchers need more data about the demographics of these populations, improved methods for collecting and analyzing data, and an increased participation of sexual and gender minorities in research. Building a more solid evidence base for LGBT health concerns will not only benefit LGBT individuals, but also add to the repository of health information we have that pertains to all people.

Hembree, Wylie C., et. al. "Endocrine Treatment of Transsexual Persons: An Endocrine Society Clinical Practice Guideline". *Journal of Clinical Endocrinology & Metabolism* 94, no. 9 (2009): 3231-3154. Accessed September 12, 2012. *https://www.endocrine.org/~/media/endosociety/Files/Publications/Clinical%20Pra ctice%20Guidelines/Endocrine-Treatment-of-Transsexual-Persons.pdf*

> OBJECTIVE: The aim was to formulate practice guidelines for endocrine treatment of transsexual persons.
> EVIDENCE: This evidence-based guideline was developed using the Grading of Recommendations, Assessment, Development, and Evaluation (GRADE) system to describe the strength of recommendations and the quality of evidence, which was low or very low.
> CONSENSUS PROCESS: Committees and members of The Endocrine Society, European Society of Endocrinology, European Society for Pediatric Endocrinology, Lawson Wilkins Pediatric Endocrine Society, and World Professional Association for Transgender Health commented on preliminary drafts of these guidelines.
> CONCLUSIONS: Transsexual persons seeking to develop the physical characteristics of the desired gender require a safe, effective hormone regimen that will 1) suppress endogenous hormone secretion determined by the person's genetic/biologic sex and 2) maintain sex hormone levels within the normal range for the person's desired gender. A mental health professional (MHP) must recommend endocrine treatment and participate in ongoing care throughout the endocrine transition and decision for surgical sex reassignment. The endocrinologist must confirm the diagnostic criteria the MHP used to make these recommendations. Because a diagnosis of transsexualism in a prepubertal child cannot be made with certainty, we do not recommend endocrine treatment of prepubertal children. We recommend treating transsexual adolescents (Tanner stage 2) by suppressing puberty with GnRH analogues until age 16 years old, after which cross-sex hormones may be given. We suggest suppressing endogenous sex hormones, maintaining physiologic levels of gender-appropriate sex hormones and monitoring for known risks in adult transsexual persons. [Journal abstract]

Kendig, Newton E. and Charles E. Samuels, Jr. "Gender Identity Disorder Evaluation and Treatment". *U.S. Bureau of Prisons*. Memorandum for Chief Executive Officers, May 31, 2012.
*http://nicic.gov/Library/025522*

> A memorandum regarding the evaluation and treatment of inmates with Gender Identity Disorder (GID) is presented. It is to be immediately implemented in response to a lawsuit settled with Vanessa Adams, a FEDERAL Bureau of Prisons (BOP) inmate at FMC Butler (NC) who has GID. "In summary, inmates in the custody of the Bureau with a possible diagnosis of GID will receive a current individualized assessment and evaluation. Treatment options will not be precluded solely due to level of services received, or lack of services, prior to incarceration" (p. 2). In other words, this memorandum ends the BOP's previous "freeze frame" policy which allowed only that treatment a person with GID was receiving before incarceration.

Lee, Alvin. "Trans Models in Prison: The Medicalization of Gender Identity and the Eighth Amendment Right to Sex Reassignment Therapy." *Harvard Journal of Law & Gender* 31(2008): 447-471.
*http://nicic.gov/Library/026530*

> The right of transgender prisoners to get sex reassignment therapy while incarcerated is explained. "Through this examination, it argues that the criticisms of a medicalized conception of gender identity are either generally refutable or irrelevant to the trans-specific prison health care context. It goes on to argue that employing such a medicalized conception is both justified and compelled by unique aspects of the prison context" (p. 450). This article is divided into the following parts: introduction; trans models' the medical model and its origins and current application, the medical model and the law, criticisms of the medical model, and the self-determinative model; the Eighth Amendment background and application to trans prisoners' right to sex reassignment therapy; defending the medical model in the prison health care context' refuting criticisms of and affirmative arguments for the medical model; and conclusion' for broad-based advocacy.

"Lesbian, Gay, Bisexual, Transgender." American Psychological Association. Accessed January 28, 2015.
*http://www.apa.org/topics/lgbt/index.aspx*

> This psychology topic webpage contains resources on "Understanding Sexual Orientation and Gender Identity". These resources come in the

form of answers to questions, places to get help, news, articles, books, and APA offices and programs.

Lewis, Don. "Gender Identity Disorder". U.S. Bureau of Prisons. Webinar and transcript, March 27, 2012.
*http://nicic.gov/Library/025870*

Issues related to gender identity are discussed. Gender identity is 'a person's sense of their own gender, which is communicated to others by their gender expression.' Objectives for this presentation are: define key terms related to Gender Identity Disorder (GID); review the diagnostic criteria for GID); implement the Bureau's new GID policy; review the history of transgender issues, to include relevant legal issues; identify World Professional Organization for Transgendered Health (WPATH) standards of care for GID; and review co-occurring disorders commonly associated with GID.

Mallon, Gerald P. 2010. LGBTQ Youth Issues: A Practical Guide for Youth Workers, Serving Lesbian, Gay, Bisexual, Transgender, and Questioning Youth. Revised Edition. CWLA Press (Washington, DC).

This book is designed to help youth care providers increase their knowledge about and skills in working with lesbian, gay, bisexual, transgender, and questioning (LGBTQ) youth and their families" (p. 9). It should also be required ready for anyone working with justice-involved youth. Twelve chapters follow and introduction to preparing for working with LGBTQ youth and an explanation of terms. These chapters are: the basics; the coming out process; family issues; discrimination and anti-LGBTQ harassment and violence; creating healthy and affirming social environments; relationships and dating; school issues; health and mental health issues for LGBTQ youth; out-of-home programs for LGBTQ youth; working with transgender and gender variant youth; other special populations within the community of LGBTQ youth; and conclusions—a call for organizational transformation. [Author abstract]

"National Healthcare Disparities Report: 2011". U.S. Department of Health and Human Services. Agency for Healthcare Research and Quality. Accessed July 15, 2012.
*http://www.ahrq.gov/research/findings/nhqrdr/nhdr11/nhdr11.pdf*

This annual report, mandated by Congress, focuses on ""prevailing disparities in health care delivery as it relates to racial factors and socioeconomic factors in priority populations". Chapter 10 contains a section on "Lesbian, Gary, Bisexual, and Transgender Populations".

*A Provider's Introduction to Substance Abuse Treatment for Lesbian, Gay, Bisexual, and Transgender Individuals.* Rockville, MD: U.S. Dept. of Health and Human Services. Substance Abuse and Mental Health Services Administration (SAMHSA). Center for Substance Abuse Treatment. 2010.
*http://nicic.gov/Library/026764*

> "This publication presents information to assist providers in improving substance abuse treatment for lesbian, gay, bisexual, and trans-gender (LGBT) clients by raising awareness about the issues unique to LGBT clients. Sensitizing providers to these unique issues will, it is hoped, result in more effective treatment and improved treatment outcomes. Effective treatment with any population should be sensitive and culturally competent. Substance abuse treatment providers, counselors, therapists, administrators, and facility directors can be more effective in treating LGBT clients when they have a better understanding of the issues LGBT clients face. With this knowledge, treatment providers can reexamine their treatment approaches and take steps to accommodate LGBT clients" (p. xiii). Sections following an executive summary are: an overview for providers treating LGBT clients; cultural issues in working with LGBT individuals; legal issues; overview of treatment approaches, modalities, and issues of accessibility in the continuum of care; the coming out process for lesbians and Gay men; families of origin and families of choice; clinical issues with lesbians; clinical issues with Gay male clients; clinical issues with bisexuals; clinical issues with transgender individuals; clinical issues with youth; related health issues; counselor competencies in treating LGBT clients; outline of pertinent policies and procedures; training and education; quality improvement and LGBT clients; using alliances and networks to improve treatment for lesbian, Gay, bisexual, and transgender clients; and recommendations.

"Scope of Services for the Treatment of Gender Identity Disorder". Colorado Department of Corrections. Administrative Regulation 700-14, Last modified November 1, 2009.
*http://www.doc.state.co.us/sites/default/files/ar/0700_14.pdf*

> "It is the purpose of this administrative regulation (AR) to serve as a standard of care for the treatment of gender identity disorder and define the extent and general limits of health services that will be provided to this population" (p.1). Procedures cover: relative contraindications; Gender Identity Disorder Management and Treatment Committee; sexual reassignment treatment; other treatment modalities; and facility

placement.

Scott, Ann V. and Rick Lines. "Final Report: HIV/AIDS in the Male-To-Female Transsexual and Transgendered Prison Population: A Comprehensive Strategy". May 1999. Accessed September 11, 2012. *http://www.pasan.org/Toolkits/T-S_%26_T-G_in_Prison.pdf*

> Since 1993, PASAN has worked with over 200 HIV positive prisoners from across Canada. Approximately 10% of PASAN's HIV positive clients identify as transsexual or transgendered (TS/TG). This experience has led us to document many specific barriers faced by TS/TG prisoners living with HIV/AIDS in accessing proper HIV/AIDS care and other support services. This brief has been produced in an attempt to identify these specific and significant issues, and recommend solutions. [Abstract from Introduction]

"Sexual Violence & Individuals Who Identify as LGBTQ Information Packet". National Sexual Violence Center". National Sexual Violence Resource Center. Accessed January 16, 2015. *http://www.nsvrc.org/publications/nsvrc-publications-information-packets/sexual-violence-individuals-who-identify-lgbtq*

> Sexual violence & individuals who identify as LGBTQ is an information packet containing nearly a dozen resources focused on serving, engaging, and collaborating with individuals and communities who identify as lesbian, gay, bisexual, transgender, queer or questioning (LGBTQ). The packet contains resources to support counselors, advocates, preventionists, technical assistance providers, and allied professionals committed to affirming all individuals and communities. The goals of this packet it to provide resources that will both strengthen work already being done, as well as assist organizations in discovering a place to begin program development. [Publisher abstract]

"Standards of Care for the Health of Transsexual, Transgender, and Gender Nonconforming People". 7th Version. World Professional Association for Transgender Health Inc. Accessed September 12, 2012. *http://nicic.gov/Library/025747*

> "The overall goal of the SOC [Standards of Care] is to provide clinical guidance for health professionals to assist transsexual, transgender, and gender nonconforming people with safe and effective pathways to achieving lasting personal comfort with their gendered selves, in order to maximize their overall health, psychological well-being, and self-fulfillment." While this is primarily a document for health professionals,

the SOC may also be used by individuals, their families, and social institutions to understand how they can assist with promoting optimal health for members of this diverse population" (p. 1). Sections of this publication are: purpose and use of the SOP; global applicability; the difference between gender nonconformity and gender dysphoria; assessment and treatment of children and adolescents with gender dysphoria; mental health; hormone therapy; reproductive health; voice and communication therapy; surgery; postoperative care and follow-up; lifelong prevention and primary care; applicability of SOP to people living in institutional environments; and applicability of SOP to people with disorders of sex development.

"Talking About Suicide & LGBT Populations." *Gay & Lesbian Alliance Against Defamation and Movement Advancement Project*. Accessed July 17, 2012. *http://www.lgbtmap.org/file/talking-about-suicide-and-lgbt-populations.pdf*

> This guide provides ways to talk about suicide more safely, while advancing vital public discussions about preventing suicide, helping increase acceptance of LGBT people, and supporting their well-being.

U.S. Department of Health & Human Services (HHS). "LGBT Health and Well-Being." Accessed January 20, 2015. *http://www.hhs.gov/lgbt/resources/reports/health-objectives-2011.html*

> A summary of the efforts taken by the U.S. Department of Health and Human Services (HHS) to improve the lives of lesbian, gay, bisexual and transgender (LGBT) people, as well as recommendations for future action.

U.S. Department of Justice. Office on Violence Against Women (OVW). "Recommendations for Administrators of Prisons, Jails, and Community Confinement Facilities for Adapting the U.S. Department of Justice's A National Protocol for Sexual Assault Medical Forensic Examinations, Adults/Adolescents." August 2013. *http://www.justice.gov/sites/default/files/ovw/legacy/2013/08/12/confinement-safe-protocol.pdf*

> "This guide is designed to assist administrators of prisons, jails, and community confinement facilities in drafting or revising protocols for an immediate response to reports of sexual assault. Sexual assault is a persistent problem in correctional environments with life-altering consequences for victims as well as for the integrity of correctional institutions and the fundamental principles of justice. The U.S. Department

of Justice's National Standards to Prevent, Detect, and Respond to Prison Rape set minimum requirements for correctional facilities to increase their overall capacity to address the problem of sexual assault. This guide is intended to help these facilities comply with the Prison Rape Elimination Act (PREA) standards, which require correctional agencies to (1) follow a uniform evidence protocol when responding to sexual assault, which as appropriate is based on the U.S. Department of Justice's A National Protocol for Sexual Assault Medical Forensic Examinations: Adults/Adolescents, (referred to in this guide as the National Protocol), and (2) coordinate responses to sexual assault among involved professionals."